WHY VIETNAM STILL MATTERS

The War and The Wall

COMPILED BY
JAN CRAIG SCRUGGS

Printed in the United States of America.
First Edition.

Photo Credits:
Front Cover, "'Roses' Requiem for Black Granite" by
Michael John Coleman
Back Cover, "Name Rubbing" by Libby Hatch

This book is dedicated to America's high school students. While it is difficult to imagine, each of you could find yourselves on a battlefield. The forces of history will determine this. It is therefore imperative that you learn the significance of what has come before. For as George Santayana once wrote . . .

> "Those who cannot remember the past are condemned to repeat it."

Value reading and learn to think.

Jan Craig Scruggs

We wish to thank:

Libby Hatch for her efforts at editing and organizing Why Vietnam Still Matters. Libby actually found and corrected more errors in the submitted articles than I did. Therefore, she did more editing. Libby made enormous efforts to motivate several tardy writers and kept on top of the many last minute problems which inevitably accompany an endeavor such as this.

Kirsten Sanda for her valuable assistance in layout and design of the book.

Alex Chadwick of the National Public Radio for his indefatigable counsel.

Special thanks go to the photographer, Michael John Coleman, for the beautiful cover photograph, "'Roses' Requiem for Black Granite." A national award winning professional photographer, Michael is also the executive director of M.A.G.N.U.M., Migraine Awareness Group: A National Understanding for Migraineurs, and is very active in promoting education about Migraine disease and helping its sufferers. Michael points out that "Both nonprofit organizations, the VVMF and the M.A.G.N.U.M., work towards the goals of lessening the suffering of Americans by utilizing the arts, communications, and education to understand the pain of others to allow for a healing process to begin."

Congratulations to Larry Levine for winning the contest to name the book.

TABLE OF CONTENTS

Page

Introduction

The War

Bud Alley 1
Peter Arnett 4
Ken Berez 6
Jim Bohannon 7
Peter Braestrup 10
Bob Canape 12
Philip Caputo 13
Kieu Chinh 14
Alex Chadwick 16
Gil Coronado 19
Country Joe McDonald 22
Kenneth Coskey 23
Tony Diamond 25
John Dibble 27
Lee Ewing 30
Duery Felton 33
Joe Galloway 35
Ron Gibbs 37
Hershel Gober 39
Elizabeth Louise Kahn 41
Rod Kane 44
Stanley Karnow 46
Michael Leaveck 48
Marc Leepson 51
Violet Long 53
George McGovern 56
John McNeill 58
Larry McQuillan 61
James Meek 63
Shad Meshad 66
Janice Nark 69
Erika Niedowski 71

Page

Terrence O'Donnell 73
Peter Rollins 76
Mary Schaaf 78
Jack Smith 81
Barbara Sonneborn 83
Stephen Sossaman 86
John Woods, Jr. 88
George Worthington 91

The Wall
Anonymous 97
Dan Arant 99
Tom Baxter 101
John Bender 102
Frank Bosch 104
Kathy Ferguson 106
Gertrude Gerber 107
Alan Gropman 108
Libby Hatch 110
Bobbie Keith 111
Suzanne Sigona 113
Ron Stufflebean 115
Alan Wallace 116

Speech by President Jimmy Carter 118

Speech by President Ronald Reagan 122

Speech by Maya Ying Lin 125

Speech by Vice President Elect Albert Gore 126

Speech by General Colin Powell 128

INTRODUCTION

This book combines the wisdom of many great men and women. Some are famous. Others are not well known, but all have contributed their thoughts and insights on the American Tragedy of Vietnam.

Part I of Why Vietnam Still Matters asks the question: What is the most important issue for high school students to understand about the Vietnam War? We received many thoughtful responses from people ranging from retired Admirals to Pulitzer Prize winning journalists. Others who have written include men and women who served in Vietnam or whose lives were affected by that difficult period in history.

Part II of the book consists of some thoughtful and interesting entries by the Volunteer Guides who donate so much of their time at the Wall, helping veterans and other visitors at the Memorial. They have written about poignant moments, sometimes known as "Wall Magic," that occur so frequently at the Vietnam Veterans Memorial. We have also included just a handful of the many memorable speeches given at the Wall. We have held Memorial Day and Veterans Day ceremonies each year since the VVMF began its efforts in 1979. Americans ranging from sitting Presidents to Gold Star Mothers to prominent veterans have shared their insights at the patriotic observances.

This book is dedicated to high school students. Although they were born after the 1975 fall of Saigon, we want them to more fully understand how thoughtful and articulate Americans continue to disagree on the most divisive American experience of the Twentieth Century—the Vietnam War. I encourage everyone to read this book and see how it influences your perceptions of this controversial epoch in our nation's history.

Jan Craig Scruggs, Esq.
President and Founder
Vietnam Veterans Memorial Fund

A BRIEF HISTORY OF THE VIETNAM WAR

Vietnam has a nearly perpetual history of military conflict. In 1789, just a few years after American Independence, Vietnam defeated an invasion by China. France conquered Vietnam (then called Cochinchina) in 1862 when Americans were fighting in places like Gettysburgh and Bull Run during the Civil War. Vietnam was a French colony until World War II when the Japanese occupied Vietnam. After the defeat of Japan in 1945, Vietnam declared its independence.

In 1946, French troops moved back to reclaim the colony of Vietnam. The First Indochina War began with the arrival of the French and ended in 1954 with the French surrender at Dien Bien Phu. In Geneva, Switzerland, an agreement was made creating North and South Vietnam divided by the 17th Parallel. The U.S. began a program of military aid to South Vietnam, motivated by our concern about the spread of communism in Asia.

In 1959, the first two American soldiers were killed. The final casualties were on May 1975. Approximately 3,000,000 Americans served. The number of U.S. killed and missing exceeds 58,000.

Americans were primarily advisors until 1965, when combat troops landed. By 1969, over 550,000 Americans were in Vietnam. A treaty was signed in Geneva bringing about a cease fire on January 28, 1973, which allowed U.S. troops to withdraw. On April 30, 1975, the South Vietnamese government surrendered after massive battlefield defeats from the North Vietnamese Army.

American men and women fought with great valor under some of the most difficult circumstances ever faced by our military forces. Although U.S. troops were able to constantly defeat the enemy in battles, the North Vietnamese accepted the defeats believing that America would tire of the war. In the United States, the Vietnam War brought about massive demonstrations and a raging domestic controversy as the conflict continued.

WHY VIETNAM STILL MATTERS

The War

BY BUD ALLEY

What are the most important issues to understand about the Vietnam War? My friend from the Ia Drang Valley battle, Haskell Shadden, says to tell you that "freedom's not free." Stuart Pace wants to be sure you know our generation was taught that we had an obligation to serve America and we believed in "duty, honor and country." Linda Mines' American history class asks, "How did it start? Why was the war controversial? Why were there protests?"

In addressing these issues, you must know history. By looking back in time, we can often spot seeds of tomorrow's conflicts in today's peace settlements. The seeds of Vietnam's discontent were sewn in the peace of World War II as the U.S. granted France major concessions in their colonial empire in return for a "free" presence on the European continent. Vietnam was one of these colonies. Ho Chi Minh, a Vietnamese leader, rallied his country and from 1946 to 1954 they fought to overthrow the harsh colonial rule of the French. As the United Nations, led by the United States, imposed a peace settlement to end French rule, the final seeds of American direct involvement were planted. The settlement forced the country into two parts—a Communist led North and a capitalistic or free society was set up in the South. The Communist North never accepted the settlements.

As many who fought in Vietnam were growing up in the 1950s, the Cold War was very real to us. It gave us technology and the Atomic Bomb. The Communists were our clear enemy. We practiced air raid drills, learned where bomb shelters were, knew what NORAD was and which radio station to turn to in the event of national emergency. Technology brought us instant access to events around the world through telephones, radios, newspapers, and television. We went from mass transportation to a car for every family. We invented suburbs and work-easing appliances. Television brought us American Bandstand and Little Rock, Arkansas High School's integration. As the decade brought prosperity to many through technology, some were left out. By the end of the decade, TV was in color. By the end of the decade, the communists had the Sputnik satellite over our heads.

From this wealthy heritage, our generation burst into young adulthood. We were impressed by the call of J.F.K. to go anywhere and pay any price to protect freedom. College campuses were expanding rapidly, new ideas were being exchanged and formulated on them. American youth was exploring the limits of its new found freedoms. Martin Luther King was leading black Americans in search of their freedoms. James Dean was a pop icon, Motown was emerging, the Beatles were pushing decorum to new limits. Marches began on campus and the streets, and the times, "they were a'changin'." Ironically, the U.S. military was leading the changes. It was the one place you were judged by the worth of your character.

In 1964, after Lyndon Johnson had ascended to the U.S. Presidency, there was a reported incident off the shore of North Vietnam in the Gulf of Tonkin where an American ship was attacked. President Johnson with the backing of Robert McNamara, Secretary of Defense, pressed Congress for a resolution that gave him a free hand to deal with this armed threat to U.S. foreign policy. Thus, without due process, our political leaders were given a blank check to be paid for in American lives by embroiling us in the internal affairs of another nation. Greatly influenced by civilian appointees such as Robert McNamara and Dean Rusk, L.B.J. sent men to war to "protect freedom from the Communist hordes." As race relations exploded in turbulence and violence at home, our enemies in S.E. Asia exploded into South Vietnam. Johnson's tactics at home resembled his war efforts. He spent billions to buy peace when peace was not for sale.

You should know that the men who were sent to fight were loyal Americans committed to preserving freedom. We were idealistic and naive but we were following in our father's footsteps to defend freedom and liberate people from oppression. You should know that over two million American men and women served in Vietnam. You should know over 58,000 men and women gave their lives to a cause that our leaders told us was just. You should know the civilian leadership overruled many military decisions. You should know that leaders can be fallible. They should not be allowed to shrug off their responsibility lightly. They should not be allowed to profit from risking American lives. The appointees should be held accountable. You should become informed of the history you live every day. You should know that *freedom is not free.*

Near the Cambodian border in the Ia Drang Valley on November 17, 1965, two months to the day after he arrived in South Vietnam with the 1st Cavalry, Lt. Bud Alley found himself in the middle of the battle for LZ Albany as told in <u>We Were Soldiers Once . . . And Young</u> by Lt. Gen. H.G. Moore and Joe Galloway. Haskell Shadden of Tellico, TN was severely wounded in that battle. Stuart Pace, an Easley, S.C. native, was wounded in 1967 while an artillery man.

BY PETER ARNETT

The most important issue of the Vietnam War was the ability of the media and the public to gain access to the war's secrets—and in revealing them, help end the long, dark night of official dishonesty. As it was, the Vietnam War was the longest in American history. It could have lasted ad infinitum had not a vigilant press and a strong-willed citizenry successfully challenged the official view of the war.

I mentioned the "war secrets" and by these I don't mean the tactical security data governing the battlefield that of necessity needs to be protected. I am referring to the political secrets hidden by Washington bureaucrats relating to the real assessment of Vietnam in the White House during the five presidencies under which the Vietnam conflict was conducted—from the Eisenhower Administration in the 1950s to the Ford Administration in the mid 1970s.

Part of the truth was dramatically brought to light by the publication of the secret history of the war, the Pentagon Papers, in the New York Times and other newspapers in the early 1970s. What they revealed was a pattern of official deception and capriciousness over Vietnam policy, even as thousands of young Americans were dying on the battlefield and billions of dollars were being spent on the war. But long before the Pentagon Papers were published, there was a serious, dedicated commitment by American reporters in the field to bring home the truth of the war to their readers and viewers.

Because of the political sensitivity of the involvement, there was no attempt to impose press censorship in Vietnam; it was the first modern American war to allow full freedom to reporters to cover events as they saw them. Such license allowed the media not only to gain unprecedented access to the battlefield, but also to discuss sensitive military issues candidly and promptly, particularly troop morale and the battle readiness of units and their performance in the field.

The ease of access to the war—and the willingness of many reporters to accept the dangerous challenge of reporting from the front lines—allowed the media to authoritatively question the optimistic assessments routinely emanating from the White House and the Pentagon, even as casualties sharply increased and hundreds of thousands of draft age young Americans continued to be sent to Vietnam. The media reports gave energy to the emerging anti-war movement; the two combined convinced the Johnson and Nixon Administrations to bring an end to American involvement.

The war concluded disastrously in 1975 with the routing of America's South Vietnamese allies and the fall of Saigon to the communist side. In the long, angry post-mortem, some senior officers in the Pentagon chose to blame the media for not being "on the team," for questioning the official line. The senior officers suggested that the national interest required the blind endorsement of government policy by the media. In the Grenada and Panama invasions and the Gulf War, the Pentagon with White House support, reintroduced complete censorship of the press.

But in the three most recent American military commitments—Somalia, Haiti, and Bosnia—the post-Vietnam era Pentagon leadership has reassessed policy yet again and opted for free, open media coverage, whatever the consequences. By this guarantee of honesty in America's overseas commitments, the public is better served and a lesson from the Vietnam War has been well learned.

Peter Arnett covered the Vietnam War for the Associated Press from 1962 to 1975, winning the Pulitzer Prize for his reporting. Working for CNN, Arnett has since been covering numerous international crises, including the Gulf War and Bosnia, and has published an autobiography, Live From The Battlefield.

BY KEN BEREZ

High school students today need to appreciate that the generation which came of age in the 1960s grew up with a life experience that, in large part, mitigated other choices but to serve. We were the products of the last "GOOD WAR."

The question at schools that is always put to me is: How did I let myself be used and manipulated, given all the controversy surrounding the war?

My response has been that our generation, in large part, did not question authority; be it political, military, academic, religious, journalistic, etc. These were and still are the opinion-making institutions which shape public opinion on issues of national importance, right down to what information high school children receive.

A lesson of the Vietnam War, for high school teenagers of today, is to not become cynical about their world, but to maintain a healthy skepticism of the institutions referenced above. It was a hard lesson learned too late in the game by the generation that served in Vietnam.

Today's students have the "BAD WAR" of Vietnam as their model. Hopefully, this difference with the '60s generation will encourage tough questions of all levels of authority with matters that affect their young lives.

Ken Berez was an Army infantryman in Vietnam where he was seriously injured. He now works with the National Veterans Legal Services Project (NVLSP). NVLSP provides important legal representation for those who have served in the U.S. Military.

BY JIM BOHANNON

The MOST important thing for high school students to understand is the factual basis of the war. Do you know about French Indochina? Do you know about the battle of Dien Bien Phu? Do you know about the Geneva Treaty of 1954? Do you know about the escalation of the American presence from President Eisenhower through Kennedy, Johnson, and Nixon? It's been 34 years since I was in high school, so I don't know how much is taught or how well it's taught about that time and that place. For most of you, my guess is not much and not well. My guess is that most students will obtain that diploma without having to take a world history course, much less one focused on recent events in Asia. And I'll bet a week's pay that only a handful of you have even had the opportunity to take a full-fledged course in geography, much less the obligation to take it. *Find out about the Vietnam War. There are lessons to be learned which will stand you in good stead as active, informed citizens.*

Another important thing to understand is that Hollywood turns out very few documentaries. Mostly, it turns out entertainment, often without regard to the facts. Don't feel that you understand the war just because you've seen "The Green Berets," "The Deer Hunter," and "Platoon."

If you hear much at all about the Vietnam War, it'll probably include the conventional wisdom on the subject. I find much of that conventional wisdom unwise:

MYTH: The Vietnam War was a civil war.
FACT: It was a war of conquest that was planned, directed, financed, and trained by the leadership in Hanoi, in violation of the 1954 Geneva Treaty. It was, fortunately, the *last* great communist war of conquest.

MYTH: The 1968 Tet Offensive was a surprise to U.S. forces.

FACT: I served in intelligence. We knew exactly which units would be involved and roughly where they'd be coming from. By the time the first rockets hit Long Binh around 2 or 3 in the morning, the main question most of us had was, "Where are they? Did they forget it's the Tet holiday?"

MYTH: The Tet Offensive was a great communist victory.
FACT: Tet was one of the most lop-sided defeats ever inflicted on a foe by U.S. forces. Assaults were launched on scores of provincial capitals, with almost all being repelled. The attack on the U.S. Embassy in Saigon was a suicide mission which was bound to fail. Only in the old imperial city of Hue was there a communist occupation of any length. Tet virtually destroyed the Viet Cong. From that point on, almost all of the large-unit fighting was conducted by north Vietnamese regular army units.

MYTH: The Vietnam War was unwinnable.
FACT: The U.S. could have won that war any time it wanted to, and within a matter of weeks. You may debate all you want about whether or not we *should* have applied the necessary force (my view is an unqualified yes), but there is *absolutely no question* of our capabilities. We simply lacked the will to bring those resources to bear.

Clearly, these are my views, and I will defend them with anyone. The important thing is that these are views rarely heard from the revisionists of history. Before you swallow what they say, consider what I've said. And above all, as citizens who'll be leading this nation in the 21st century, learn the lesson of the Vietnam War, and of the whole bankrupt concept of "limited war": *a war worth fighting is a war worth winning. And if it isn't worth winning, it isn't worth fighting.*

Jim Bohannon, talk show host, Westwood One Radio, and SP5, 199th Brigade, April 67-68. Speaker at the Vietnam Veterans Memorial, Veterans Day, 1990.

BY PETER BRAESTRUP

I suggest that there are several things Americans should remember about the Vietnam War.

It was a war fought for noble purposes—to defend an ally from a Communist takeover. What followed after the "liberation" of Saigon confirmed the proposition that Hanoi's victory would bring great harm and distress to the South Vietnamese people; more than a million fled, risking and, too often, losing their lives in attempts to escape.

It was a war for survival for the non-Communist South Vietnamese. Less than a decade after independence from France, they were caught up in a semi-civil war in the South, against the insurgent Viet Cong, directed and increasingly re-enforced by the North. Historically, less united than the North, the South Vietnamese had no counterpart to Hanoi's war-tested Communist party organization; the fragile Saigon regimes of 1963-75 were plagued by mediocre leadership, corruption, and the class inequalities left over from the days of French rule. Even so, no South Vietnamese army unit ever went over to the foe, and close to 300,000 South Vietnamese died in battle.

The political leaders of the United States—Presidents Kennedy, Johnson, and Nixon—tried to fight the war on the "political cheap." Johnson, in particular, tried to avoid facing up to whether the defense of South Vietnam, with all its obvious costs and risks, was vital to America's interests. He did not want to be accused of "losing" South Vietnam but he did not want to forfeit his Great Society programs either. Instead, he sought initially to obfuscate America's growing Vietnam commitment. He did not ask Congress for a declaration of war or mobilize the country behind the 500,000 men he and Defense Secretary Robert McNamara slowly sent to Vietnam. Nor did he develop a firm long term strategy for success, once he committed U.S. forces. Public confusion, then demoralization ensued.

American soldiers, sailors and Marines, especially before

President Nixon began troop withdrawals in 1969, performed as well or better than their forebears in World War II or Korea. They were neither victims nor psychopaths, as portrayed by some anti-war folk and Hollywood. They were probably better disciplined than their elders. (Less damage and fewer civilian losses were inflicted on South Vietnam than on the Koreans during the 1950-53 Korean War.) In a war seemingly without end, they did their duty, while others did not.

One can argue about why Hanoi won. But geography and U.S. political constraints surely barred allied victory in 1965-73. In Washington, U.S. military leaders did not seriously challenge these constraints. Hanoi could always use Laos and Cambodia freely to re-enforce the South; U.S. forces were not allowed to block the enemy's vital Ho Chi Minh Trail through these countries. As long as the Trail was open, the North Vietnamese held the strategic initiative, choosing when to fight costly battles or fall back to their sanctuaries. Under these circumstances, supplied by the Soviets, the determined North Vietnamese could simply outlast the United States in a test of wills.

Peter Braestrup is the former Washington Post Saigon bureau chief and the author of Big Story (rev. 1994), a study of media coverage of the 1968 Tet Offensive, and Vietnam As History (1984).

BY BOB CANAPE

March fourth, 1969, I missed my spot by maybe an inch: I mean, a .50 round to the head, what do they want? With about as much life in me as an SP chocolate bar, some heroes got me in a chopper. It's 27 years later. Not a lot has changed, Jody still has the girl who ran off with him. The new ones, who never get old, they know who took arms against a sea of troubles, and that's who they want to be with. Our younger brothers are still bragging about us, and the guys who made excuses still don't really look you in the eye, still want to pat you on the back but don't feel their own smile, and we still don't really care.

You'll hear songs about us; the songs of "I don't want to go" unfortunately died off as soon as those guys didn't have to go. The wall is down in Berlin, people are in 'Nam, carrying the spirit of our effort, without letting governments or politicians or TV near. The spirit is carried, the gift of America is being shared, part of a monument to you, to us. Girls get a lot more starry eyed hearing about athletes dying young than they do hearing about politicians dying wrinkled, "and it was one, two, three, what are we fighting for?" See you, Cpl. Canape, Kilo, 3/26/96

Bob Canape was a machine gunner in I CORPS, Kilo Company, III Battalion, 26th Marines. After being injured during the first tour, he returned for a second tour of duty and on the second day was shot in the head. He lost the use of one arm, has a plate in his head, but returned and through the help of a community, has built two homes for his wife, Kathy, and cat, Ah-Ah. He talks to high school students about Vietnam and is currently writing a book about his experiences.

BY PHILIP CAPUTO

By the second century A.D., the Roman Empire extended from Britain in the north to the Nile Valley in the south, and from the Atlantic Ocean to the Tigris and Euphrates. There was a current of opinion among some Roman leaders, at that time, to expand the Empire beyond the Persian Gulf and fulfill Alexander the Great's dream to bring Persia and India permanently under the rule of Western civilization. The emperor Hadrian (who built Hadrian's Wall across northern England) was, however, skeptical about these expansionist dreams. He seemed to sense that enlarging the empire to such an extent would lead it to fall of its own weight, and he declared that Terminus, the Roman god of limits, had set the empire's eastern boundary at the Tigris and Euphrates for all time. If Lyndon Johnson, Robert McNamara, and all "the best and brightest" who led us into the catastrophe of Vietnam had read their Roman history, perhaps they would have realized that there are limits to the power of even the greatest nations and kept the troops home.

Born in 1944, Philip Caputo served in Vietnam as a Marine rifle platoon leader in 1965-66. He returned to Vietnam in 1975 as a war correspondent to cover the fall of Saigon. He is the author of A Rumor of War *and five other books, and is now at work on a collection of novellas.*

BY KIEU CHINH

Being a Vietnamese-American, who has taken refuge twice, who has lost parents and siblings and almost everything because of the war, who has fidgeted with countless questions and contradicting thoughts, please let me share with you some reflections upon the Vietnam War—looking back from the Wall.

When joining the 10th Anniversary of the Wall, reciting names of the dead, I recognized that while standing there, at this place, and commemorating in front of the huge Wall inscribed with names of over 58,000 American casualties in the Vietnam War, all reasons for the war were faded and gone.

I looked at the Wall and saw the whole humanity and globe appear as one body. This common body of humanity, just like a person growing up step by step, is sometimes healthy, wise, and sometimes sick, unwise, self-inflicted.

One of the self-inflicted wounds of humanity is called the Vietnam War.

This wound is not small. Just look at the two sides of the Pacific Ocean. On one side, a country of 320,000 kilometers square was ravaged, a people split. And on this side, numerous American generations were divided. Over 58,000 American soldiers fell, and over two million people—soldiers, civilians, the aged and the young—died in the unfortunate land chosen by history to be the battlefield. This wound is still painful for millions, decades after the silence prevailed over the guns.

Vietnam veterans, returning from the battlefield with physical or spiritual wounds, continue their battles, not for inflicting more but for healing them when taking part with American civilians to build the Wall of the Vietnam Veterans Memorial.

Within a decade, over twenty five million people have come to it. And certainly millions more will come to it.

Vietnam Veterans Memorial has never been a monument of the war, but a hope for healing. It is a place where the dead remind the living of their hopes for a more peaceful world.

History shows that all the walls erected to separate and damage humanity have collapsed. But the Wall that has brought people together for healing, in the meaning of the Vietnam Veterans Memorial, will stand forever because it's made not only of stone but also of spirit, not only to stay on earth but also to live in human hearts.

The earth, our common home, is still increasingly intimidated by the destruction of more horrible weapons.

May the message from the Wall on the Vietnam War remind future generations to learn how to keep the earth safe for humanity growing up in a body intact, healthy, and peaceful.

Kieu Chinh, a Vietnamese-American actress, appeared in about 70 movies and TV shows; the most recent ones are "The Joy Luck Club" (1993) and "Riot" (1996). She now assists the Vietnam Memorial Association, which sponsors the construction of dozens of elementary schools in Vietnam regions most ravaged by the war. These schools are considered as living monuments dedicated to the memory of over two million people who died in the war and for the benefit of future generations.

BY ALEX CHADWICK

A bullet going past your ear sounds like a bee flying at a thousand miles per hour. You don't hear the bang from the rifle. Just the fast buzz.

The people you never expect to get shot do get shot. The innocent get shot, civilian and soldier alike. (There are innocent soldiers.) In a civilized society, innocence can be a kind of shield; even bullies will defer to it. But in war, there is so much violence, so much of it random, that anyone who isn't careful all the time is liable to get crushed. It's a bad circumstance for innocence.

In any combat situation where you look different from the native people, you are at a disadvantage. The instinct of common identity is very strong; you are going to be seen as an outsider. You *are* an outsider. There are generations of family history built into daily events . . . they pass with a meaning you do not grasp. At an impossibly young age, you may have to make very serious judgments without understanding much of what is happening. Whether they are on your side or not, the native people understand events in a way that you will not. Your ignorance and your foreign-ness are the enemy's most powerful weapons.

You cannot save a people. No matter how you want to do what is best for them, no matter how much you want them to have a life as good and decent as that of most Americans, you cannot save a people. It is difficult enough to save a person; nations must find their own salvation. You will meet strong, worthy, brave and dedicated individuals in the nation you are sent to save. You will want to help them, and on a personal level you can. But you cannot make their country into a participatory democracy for them.

War is usually not dangerous. Most of the time, it's like being in school. You're young, you have friends, and there are authority figures who bug you about useless stuff. You play music, hang out, and fight boredom more than anything. But everyone is carrying a gun and, in a strange way, it makes you polite to each other. You don't want to crowd some guy in a bad mood who has a hand grenade. You're always careful.

You can do things in war that seem all right because it's war, and the rules are different. Afterwards, you'll go back to normal life. For years afterward, probably for all of your life, you'll reexamine what you did. If you ever have to go and fight, remember that. Governments don't have consciences; you do. You will have to live with your conscience. The worst casualties I've known are those who didn't understand this thirty years ago.

You can avoid the draft, but you cannot avoid your moment. If a national military crisis—real or manufactured—confronts your generation, you must participate. If you oppose the war, work against it. It does no good to get away from service, and then merely speak against the war from time to time. Others in your generation are consumed by the war. We as a nation are engaged. If you are against it, be against it full time. This division still splits my generation . . . did you go? and if you didn't, what did you do? There is no respect for those who slunk away.

War is not simply a national issue. It is a community issue. Pay attention to what people in your community are saying. It's often difficult to know which national leaders you can really believe, but you do have a pretty good idea of who is trustworthy in your neighborhood. Does the sacrifice of war seem necessary to them? Do they understand why we are fighting?

The central question for us to ask is not simply do we wish for our way to prevail in some other place, but what are we willing to do in order to see it prevail? What will it cost us in brothers and sisters? What will it cost us from our souls? What will we have to do to others? If you can understand these questions, and are able to live with the answers, and if your friends and neighbors can, then go. You are going into war with extraordinary company, with other Americans you would not otherwise meet. War may be hell, but warriors can be wonderful.

There are places you can leave that will never truly leave you.

Alex Chadwick served in Vietnam as an enlisted man from 1967 through 1968 in the Army and following military service joined the anti-war movement. He is currently a correspondent for National Public Radio.

BY GIL CORONADO

The Selective Service System is a federal government agency. It is independent of the Department of Defense, but its job—unchanged since 1940—is to provide men for involuntary service in the armed forces in case of a national emergency. There has been no actual draft since 1973, but all men in the United States that are between the ages of 18 and 25 are required, by law, to register. In a crisis, the Congress and the President could direct the System to bring forth the steps that would lead to induction.

During the Vietnam War, even though resistance to the draft grew to significant proportions, the resistance was not pervasive. The vast majority of young men registered. Between 1964 and 1973, nearly 1.8 million young men were found qualified, accepted induction, and served honorably. Further, the American public—since the inception of a national draft in World War I and the creation of the Selective Service System in 1940—has long supported the concept of the obligation for involuntary military service when world events threaten U.S. security and national interest.

Until 1965—when large-scale intervention by American combat troops began in South Vietnam—the draft was not regarded as a problem. In 1963, when the 1951-vintage draft law had come up for renewal in Congress, only 22 percent of men serving in the Army were draftees. Induction numbered about 100,000 men per year, but the pool of 19 to 25 year-old men had grown from 8 million in 1958 to 12 million in 1964. The abundance of registrants had led President Kennedy to increase the number of men deferred—more students and more married men. Only small numbers of non-volunteers were called to serve and there was no public clamor about the inequities.

This situation changed drastically as the Vietnam conflict flared. To sustain the strength of the military, President Johnson hiked draft calls, going from 16,000 to 40,000 per month. For the following three years, induction was three times what it had been in the era before the American commitment in the Southeast Asian conflict.

As the conflict escalated and the draft call remained high, public resistance to the draft increased. Even those without serious objections to the war doubted the fairness of the draft system. Much inequity was perceived as a class bias, with "unfair" occupational and student deferments allowing the rich to avoid service and forcing the poor into uniform.

Arguments about the structure of the Selective Service System centered on the make-up of Local and Appeal Boards, the uniformity in "quotas" and classification actions, and the uncertainty for the individual man of enduring eight years of "vulnerability." The Boards had existed—and functioned very well—since the Selective Service began. Aside from staffs at state and national levels, the only paid, full-time employees of the System were the secretaries and clerks who worked in hundreds of offices spread throughout the nation. A Local Board, typically, served the population of an entire county in rural areas or parts of a populous county or city. The Board members, the people who actually considered and decided on problems of classification, deferment or exemption, were uncompensated volunteers from the communities—neighbors, who in good conscience, decided the fate of young men who were their neighbors. Problems in structure were symptoms of the fact that the Vietnam War was an undeclared conflict—and when stressed by unplanned demands, the old ways broke down.

Recommendations for reform came from several commissions appointed by either the President or the Congress between 1967 and 1970. In 1969, Congress granted the President authority to conduct a lottery drawing in selecting men for induction, rather than the prevailing systems which took the oldest available men first. Under new regulations implementing this lottery system, registrants would spend just one year in the first priority group available for induction, and within this group their birth dates openly ranked the likelihood of being called to serve. In the next two years, more changes followed: most deferments were abolished; a uniform national call was instituted; and legislation was enacted that set new regulations for Local and Appeal Boards.

Then, in 1971, legislation provided that the Selective Service would continue to exist—in a "stand-by status"—even if induction ended. Induction ended in 1973. The requirement for men to register ended in 1975. In 1980, President Carter reinstated registration only without a draft. Today, men must register when they reach the age of 18 years; there is no draft. However, in a national crisis, the law provides for quick restoration of the steps of classification, examination, and induction. A sudden threat to national security of a magnitude beyond the capabilities of the small existing active and reserve military force could again make the draft a reality for young men. Selective Service remains true to its purpose of providing America with the manpower the armed forces may deem necessary, through a fair and equitable process.

Gil Coronado retired from the United States Air Force in 1989 as a Colonel, after serving his country for thirty years. He is a high school "drop out" who through hard work and perseverance, has achieved his highest goals. Mr. Coronado was appointed by President Clinton and approved by the Senate to serve as the ninth Director of the Selective Service System.

BY COUNTRY JOE MCDONALD

It is important for you to know that *high school students* fought the Vietnam War. The average age of the Vietnam War soldier was *19 years old.* Many soldiers were 17 or 18 years old. And although more than 50% of the 10 million boys and girls and men and women who were in the military during the war *volunteered*, the rest were *drafted.*

Drafted means: GO TO WAR OR GO TO JAIL!

You also need to know that it was America's longest war. The Vietnam War *lasted over 15 years!*

Many of the people who died fighting the Vietnam War had *never reached their 21st birthdays.* They never got to be a grown-up . . . You can relate to that.

People in the military are governed by a different set of laws than civilians. It is called the Uniform Code of Military Justice: The UCMJ. And the military contract you sign is almost impossible for you to break without terrible consequences. That contract is protected by the United States Supreme Court which ruled that *military personnel can't sue the military.* The contract can also be changed at any time, but only by the government.

Today, most leaders, citizens and historians think the Vietnam War was a mistake from day one.

Given this, boys and girls, I ask you to think on this . . .

What if the war is wrong? And you are asked to fight? What if it's a "bad war"?

Will people blame you for what happens? And does the rest of the country have the right to ask you to take the chance?

Country Joe McDonald, ATC3, USN, 1959–62. Country Joe wrote and performed the anti-Vietnam War anthem "I Feel Like I'm Fixin' To Die Rag" at Woodstock. In 1995, he and the City of Berkeley, CA dedicated a memorial plaque to the 22 Berkeley citizens who died in Vietnam.

BY KENNETH COSKEY

The most important issue for high school students to understand about the Vietnam War is that the goals and intentions of the United States government and the U.S. military were *honorable*.

The political atmosphere during the period between the end of World War II and the beginning of our direct military involvement in Vietnam, in the early '60s, was one of constant tension between the communist countries and the free world. The United States military was the *only* force strong enough to prevent a complete step-by-step domination of all free world governments.

North Vietnam was *perceived* to be a part of this total communist effort toward political/military control. The communist regimes were making inroads in Asia, Africa, and Europe. It was decided to "draw the line" in Vietnam.

The weak, corrupt government in South Vietnam, the errors in judgment by the U.S. government concerning the determination of the North Vietnamese, and the rapid change of the American people from support to almost total disillusionment with the war all contributed to the failure of the effort by our government to prevent the eventual defeat of South Vietnam.

Those Americans that were asked by their country to fight, and accepted this call to duty, made the right choice. Those that ran away to Canada or dodged the draft in some other way, will have to live with their decision for the rest of their lives.

In 1816, in a toast at a dinner in Norfolk, Virginia, an American naval hero, Stephen Decatur, said, "Our country: in her intercourse with foreign nations may she always be in the right; but our country, right or wrong!" It should not, of course, be inferred from this that a military person should blindly follow illegal orders. And, in hindsight, our government made costly errors in the prosecution of the war. But when our elected President calls for a military response, the military must act immediately, with little question. Otherwise, our form of government will not stand for long.

Kenneth Coskey was a Naval Aviator, Commander of an A-6 squadron in combat. When his aircraft was disabled, he was captured by the North Vietnamese in 1968, and spent five years as a Prisoner of War. He is presently Executive Director of the Naval Historical Foundation in Washington, D.C.

BY TONY DIAMOND

Wars end and men and women come home from them, but will the Vietnam veteran ever really return from his or her war is the question we continually ask ourselves. Will we ever be able to forget those sacrifices and our service, those we served with, and those still unaccounted for? Will we ever be able to forgive our fellow Americans for the treatment we received upon our return?

There are many of us who served our country and feel that America let us down. We offered our lives in sacrifice and service because we believed we were following in the footsteps of the freedom fighters who had gone on before us. And there are those who served since, and those serving today, in Bosnia and many other unforgiving places. We and they answered the call.

Who are we, the veterans? What makes us different? Why can't we just forget about the war and go on with our lives? All logical questions, but there is no logic in war. For many, the Vietnam War came at an impressionable time in our lives. The average age of the serviceman in Vietnam was 19 years old. We thought we had grown up enough to know what life was all about. Our country called and we answered the call. Whether we volunteered or were drafted, we answered the call.

Just as our forefathers did, we believed our country was right. Old Glory was the banner we held high. Why was the Vietnam War different from the wars that came before, like the great patriotic war, World War II? Vietnam was a different time, a different place. I relate the Vietnam War as too many wars too soon, too many heroes too quick.

There have been many books written, fact and fiction, many words said and still more dialogue to come. There are many things we have learned, but there is only one conclusion. Another Vietnam must never happen again. Another mother's son or daughter should never again die in war. Another brother or sister should not be just a memory as one who gave his or her life so that others might live. Honor those whose names are now on the Wall and honor those who served and serve today. In a perfect world, there should never be another war, but we do not live in a perfect world. The honor you give to them will be the honor you may someday receive.

Tony Diamond, Korean War veteran and veteran of four tours in Vietnam as a USO entertainer, is the Chief Executive Officer and co-founder of BRAVO—Brotherhood Rally of All Veterans Organizations—the world-wide media organization for military and veteran affairs. He has been an active participant in veterans affairs for 25 years.

BY JOHN C. DIBBLE

I came back from Vietnam in the summer of 1971. It was several years before anyone asked, or even wanted to know, if I'd been in the war. It was also about that long before I volunteered the information. It was just a matter of practical necessity: you could never be sure how the person you were talking to felt about Vietnam, and by the time you found out, it was usually too late. Most veterans, and I was one of them, didn't say anything at all.

It was some time after the fall of Saigon in 1975 that Vietnam slowly, but surely, began to be an acceptable topic of conversation. People began to ask, with what seemed genuine interest, if I had been in the war. But during these conversations, I also began to notice a very peculiar thing. About every third or fourth person would then ask, "Were you wounded?"

I was not, in fact, wounded in Vietnam. Simply a matter of luck, as any veteran will tell you. But I thought it odd that people would, out of nowhere, ask me that question. Just as odd, when I told them I had not been wounded, it usually ended the conversation as far as they were concerned.

When this conversational oddity first began, I didn't know how to react. At first, I was a bit hurt by the question. Maybe, by not being wounded, I was viewed as not *really* having been in the war. But the more times I was asked the question and the more I thought about it, the more clear it became that the question really had nothing to do with me.

Keep in mind that these odd conversations took place in settings about as far removed from war as you can imagine—settings like a Midwest university campus or a neighborhood social gathering. There I was, a twenty-something young man who looked like a lot of other twenty-something young men. People, I decided, had a difficult time putting me together with a war that had appeared on their televisions every night for years and had, quite literally, torn this country apart. I decided that the question about whether I had been wounded was spawned by the fact that, for many people, the war so defied understanding that they needed some physical manifestation—a wound—to help them comprehend it.

I think that the people who asked this question never understood that Vietnam wounded more than just the combatants. Of course, by saying that I don't mean to lessen the tragedy of those who actually suffered physical and mental wounds in Vietnam. Those are the wounds that can't be hidden and don't have to be explained. But wars in general, and Vietnam in particular, take their toll in other, less obvious ways.

When I graduated from college in 1968, the draft was in full swing. By graduation day, almost every man in my class had received a notice to report for a pre-induction physical. Of course, we never actually had a graduation day, because the campus was closed down by anti-war demonstrators. A few months later, I reported for duty in the Navy, but some of my classmates never reported to the military at all. Instead, their opposition to the war took them to Canada, or Sweden, or prison. Things were like that in 1968.

While I was in the Navy, campus demonstrations became more frequent and political opposition to Vietnam more vocal. One day in 1970, some ill-guided Ohio National Guard troops opened fire on unarmed demonstrators at Kent State University. People all across America were forced to come to grips with the effect the war was having on their children and their nation. By the time I came back from Vietnam in 1971, serious, debilitating wounds had been inflicted on the whole country.

In 1982, the Vietnam Veterans Memorial was dedicated on the Mall in Washington. Like everything else to do with the war, it was controversial. Critics of the Wall derisively called it a "black gash of shame and sorrow." They were partly right, but not for the reasons they thought. The Wall was, in fact, a wound—the wound that the whole country had suffered. It was the physical manifestation that so many people—people like those that had been asking me the question—had been looking for.

For those of us who were in Vietnam, the Wall was something different. It held the names of friends and comrades who died there. But, at that level, a memorial can only exist for those who have participated in the conflict. A truly great memorial—and the Wall is certainly that—must exist at many levels and so minister to those who were wounded in other ways.

People still ask me the question from time to time, although not as often as they did before the Wall. When they used to ask me, I would reply, "No, I was lucky. I wasn't wounded." Now I say to those who ask the question, "Everybody was wounded in Vietnam . . . *everybody*."

John C. Dibble served in Vietnam as officer-in-charge of a U.S. Navy Swift Boat and as commanding officer and senior advisor at Operating Base Kien An in the U Minh Forest. He now practices law in Washington, D.C.

BY LEE EWING

In learning about the Vietnam War, remember this if nothing else: images can deceive.

When you think of the end of the war, what picture do you see? If you are like many Americans, it is that of a helicopter atop the U.S. Embassy in Saigon, where an ant-like file of evacuees clambers up a ladder to board a flight to safety. The photograph, reproduced in countless books and television specials, may suggest that American combat troops fled for their lives before the onslaught of the Vietnamese Communists, who seized Saigon on April 30, 1975.

Remember that date, because it was two years *after* the last U.S. combat forces left the country. Two years.

The soldiers who were sent to Vietnam were told they were needed there to defend the people of South Vietnam from the Viet Cong and North Vietnamese. For more than ten long and bloody years, the U.S. troops fought with great skill, courage and dedication. They were not defeated on the battlefield, nor were they driven from Vietnam by military force. They were withdrawn by their civilian leaders after many Americans concluded that continued military operations were not worth the cost in lives, dollars, and political capital.

In the Tet Offensive of 1968, Americans were shocked to see North Vietnamese troops penetrate the U.S. Embassy and to learn that nearly every allied base had been attacked. The dramatic television images seemed to show that Americans were powerless against the enemy. But they did not show that actually the U.S. and its allies virtually destroyed the Viet Cong and forced North Vietnamese forces to withdraw to border sanctuaries to regroup. There they stayed, rarely venturing forth in strength while large numbers of U.S. troops remained.

While historians now agree that the 1968 Tet Offensive was a devastating military defeat for the Communists, the political shockwave it created ravaged public support for the war. The American people decided that they no longer wanted to participate in the war. President Richard Nixon fulfilled his campaign pledge to withdraw U.S. troops, leaving South Vietnam to face North Vietnam. "Vietnamization" was the term used for the U.S. policy of withdrawing troops while providing training and weapons to the Saigon government.

In the years between the 1968 Tet Offensive and the 1973 completion of the phased U.S. withdrawal, combat continued in the jungles and mountains, but major enemy forces had been cleared from the coast and plains where most South Vietnamese lived.

In 1974, a year after the last U.S. troops had gone home, the South Vietnamese fought hard and well, aided by U.S. air support, weapons and supplies, in blunting a major North Vietnamese offensive.

A year later, the North Vietnamese army invaded the South with 17 divisions. This was no raid by a band of poorly equipped guerrillas but a conventional attack by a powerful army supported by tanks, artillery and even aircraft.

The South Vietnamese armed forces, virtually crippled by a cutoff in U.S. military aid by the U.S. Congress and demoralized by America's change of heart, collapsed. The North Vietnamese and remnants of the Viet Cong rolled through the South with astounding speed until they had raised their flags over the palace in Saigon. At the end, the U.S. had only a few advisors, diplomats and security guards in the capital, so Marines were dispatched from ships offshore to evacuate them as the enemy advanced.

The real story of America's involvement in Vietnam is a tale of both mindless folly and selfless heroism, but it is far more complicated than the stark and deceptively simple image of the helicopter on the Embassy roof.

Lee Ewing served in Vietnam from 1966–1967 as a MACV intelligence advisor in Hue and from 1968–69 as a combat intelligence officer with the 101st Airborne Division. As a reporter and editor, he covered military affairs for 25 years. He has been editor of four newspapers, including Army Times and Air Force Times, and was a historical consultant to Time Life Books on a multi-volume history, "The Vietnam Experience." Currently, he is content director of Military City Online, the interactive service of the Army Times Publishing Co. on America Online (AOL) and the WorldWideWeb. Lee was instrumental in putting the "Virtual" Vietnam Veterans Memorial online. (To access on AOL, KEYWORD: WALL; to access on the Web, "http://www.militarycity.com")

BY DUERY FELTON

I am mesmerized by a photograph from the Vietnam Veterans Memorial Collection, which is composed of articles that are left at the Vietnam Veterans Memorial. This photograph is marked "Platoon 3, Fort Wood Missouri, 18 Jan 1969" and shows six rows of cleanly shaven, smiling new recruits standing at ease. These ram rod-straight troops looking at me through the years, forever young and alive, define the Vietnam War as America's first teenage war. The average age of a Vietnam-era recruit was 19, compared with 26 during World War II and 25 during the American Civil War. Only males were subject to the draft: however, there were approximately 7,500 female military personnel who served in Vietnam and eight of their names are inscribed on the Vietnam Veterans Memorial. Civilian women also were killed during the war, and during the last days, 37 female civilian employees were killed in an Air Force evacuation mission.

I want you to think of all the people in your life: your parents, siblings, cousins, aunts, uncles, friends and antagonists. The emotions evoked by your interactions with them are no different from the emotions evoked in the lives of Vietnam-era individuals or in the lives of individuals from any other era. Every casualty had concentric circles of effect, from the actual death, to the effect on loved ones, associates, acquaintances, and so on into history. The experience of the war was not the same for all participants. Year of service, area of operation, branch of service, military duties, and location of homecoming were among the factors determining the difference of experience.

Twenty one years after America's involvement in Vietnam ended with the 1975 fall of Saigon, the Vietnam War is reaching into another generation. This emerging generation is asking questions. People come to the Vietnam

Veterans Memorial to apologize, to communicate, to eulogize, and to commemorate. The tangible expressions of these needs have become the Vietnam Veterans Memorial Collection, and this collection, which is a repository of donor testimonies to the fallen and a celebration of life, may answer some questions.

Duery Felton, Jr. is the curator of the National Park Service/National Capital Area's administered Vietnam Veterans Memorial Collection (VVMC). He was drafted and served in Vietnam's III Corps with the U.S. Army's 1st Infantry Division, as a nineteen-year old platoon radio-telephone-operator. Gravely wounded, he has spent nearly 30 years undergoing rehabilitative surgeries. He has been associated with the VVMC for approximately 10 years, and has been instrumental in formulating VVMC policies, directing VVMC museum exhibitions, assisting researchers and other museum organizations, aiding in VVMC publications, and interacting with the press. He has also testified before Congress concerning veterans' issues.

BY JOE GALLOWAY

Teenagers today may find it hard to get the straight story on what happened to America and the Americans during the Vietnam War, and why. Vietnam tore a generation of Americans apart and, for many, the scars run deep and the emotions still run hot even now, 30 years later.

Perhaps others will help you sort out the political tangle of how we drifted into war in Vietnam and how we got out, so far short of victory, and what all of that did to us as a nation and a people. I want to tell you about the soldiers who fought that war, the best and the most honorable friends of my life, and why you ought to care for and about them.

The fighting, killing and dying in the Vietnam War was done, for the most part, by teenagers in the youngest Army the United States has ever sent to war. Average age of the soldier was 19, which means many were only 17 and 18 when they were sent to fight a war.

These young men, boys really, were sent off to spend their tour of duty, one year, 365 days, in the harsh heat and jungle environment of a strange land where war had been a way of life for 4,000 years. The cultural differences were overwhelming; the political questions unanswerable; the why(s) unknowable.

What was constant was the danger all around, and the bonds that tied the young GI to a few comrades close around him. His life was in their hands. Nothing else and no one else mattered. All differences—of race, class, religion, region, education—were simply set aside or ignored. The odds against survival in combat were too great to permit artificial differences to get in the way.

By day and night they lived, ate, slept, marched together through the boring hours and the terrifying moments of war. When that bond was broken, by death in combat, it was traumatic. Look at the tears on the faces of middle-aged men standing before a particular panel of the

Vietnam Veterans Memorial today, staring at one special name. They weep for someone who was closer than a brother, someone who helped them keep watch through the darkest nights, someone who may have stopped the bullet or the grenade that was meant for them. They weep for someone who was, for a few terrible months, the difference between life and death for them; someone who could never be replaced in their lives, and never was.

All wars are generally a confession of failure—the failure of society to find some other more appropriate way to resolve disputes than by sending 19-year-old boys out to kill other 19-year-old boys with rifles—and Vietnam certainly fits that mold. I argue only in favor of the humanity, and yes even the nobility, of the 19-year-old boys we sent to fight in Vietnam. We asked far too much of kids just out of high school when we threw them into the cauldron of combat, and when they came home we, as a country, turned our backs on them. Shame on us.

Joseph L. Galloway, a senior writer for U.S. News & World Report*, served more than two years as a war correspondent in Vietnam. He is co-author of the best-selling Vietnam history* We Were Soldiers Once . . . And Young.

BY RON GIBBS

The Vietnam era should be remembered as a period in history that brought about major political and social change in America. At the time of the Vietnam War, our country was in the midst of the civil rights movement which sought to bring about equal opportunity and social justice for minorities and women in America. It was the period of the Great Society where the federal government implemented major new social legislation that would have a profound impact on future generations.

Major health care, education, jobs and civil rights programs were established for all Americans. Major legislation was pushed by President Lyndon Johnson creating the Medicare and Medicaid programs to assist the elderly and poor. Headstart programs were created to educate the disadvantage children; job training programs were established to raise employment for the inner cities; and the Voting Rights Act was passed to guarantee minorities the right to vote.

In the midst of all of the political and social turmoil in the late 1960s, the Vietnam War continued to escalate with no clear strategy as to how we would win the war. It was the period when our nation saw the assassinations of Senator Robert Kennedy and civil rights leader Dr. Martin Luther King. It was the time of the Tet Offensive in Vietnam and the riots at the Democratic convention in Chicago. Ultimately, the continued national demonstrations and growing public resentment against the war toppled President Johnson and caused him to not seek the Presidential nomination in 1968.

A significant lesson from Vietnam is that our political leaders should not deceive the American people through misrepresentation or lying about our objectives and mission in war. Political leaders should be open and honest about our international goals and objectives before we send our troops off to battle. President Johnson allowed the war to escalate and deceived the members of Congress and the public about our mission and the actual number of troops in Vietnam, as well as the number of American casualties.

Furthermore, our nation has learned from Vietnam that we can never abandon our young men and women when we send them off to war. Those who fought in Vietnam and in other conflicts should be recognized for their service to our country. It does not matter whether the war was right or wrong. Individuals responded to the call from their country to serve in the military and should be remembered with dignity and honor.

The legacy from Vietnam is that our political leaders should never engage in a military conflict unless it is in the clear interest of the American people and that we have a clearly defined mission, goal, and timetable. The United States must continue to play a role internationally to maintain peace in the world, but we must do it in concert with other nations as we seek to enforce agreed upon peace accords.

Ron Gibbs served as an Army Infantry Captain from 1968–1972, and was in Vietnam from 1971–1972. He is a former candidate for U.S. Senate from Illinois and is currently a public affairs consultant in Chicago.

BY HERSHEL W. GOBER

The Vietnam War was complex, as well as controversial. There were many issues involved in the struggle for a free and democratic society for the South Vietnamese people. America was asked to help in that pursuit, and we sent the best fighting force our nation had at the time.

A couple of factors should be pointed out to anyone studying the history of the war in Vietnam. First, the U.S. military did not lose the war. Quite the contrary. Even with one hand tied behind their backs by "no-fire" buffer zones and the like, military units were extremely effective in uncovering, engaging and destroying an enemy that almost always chose to fight only on its own terms. There were no front and rear lines of battle like that of World War II. With the Tet (Vietnamese New Year) offensive and counter offensives of 1968, the Viet Cong (VC) was essentially eliminated as an effective fighting force. Once the South Vietnamese communist VC was defeated, the war effort from the North became the sole burden of the North Vietnamese Army (NVA). A more seasoned, professional and highly-trained army than the VC, even the NVA could not have stood up to the overwhelming air support and firepower of the U.S. forces. It was only through political micro-management that the effectiveness of U.S. forces was hampered and eventually brought into question.

The second factor is the exaggerated picture of events created by television media. Vietnam was the first war covered by TV crews which sent home very sharp portrayals of events almost as soon as they unfolded. Unfortunately, as is the general nature of the news media, they almost always leaned toward pictures and stories of the more sensational and dire nature. The Tet offensive is a good example. A tremendous American military victory, yet the TV people zeroed in on sending home stories showing dead U.S. personnel near the Embassy, horrifying pictures, and created the impression that it was a severe blow to the U.S. and the South Vietnamese. The effect was so strong that American opposition against the war at home increased dramatically, and the political meddling in military operations began to have a greater negative impact than ever before.

There were so many lessons learned from the Vietnam War, it's not possible to list them all here. But maybe the greatest one, and one which we saw applied during the Persian Gulf War, is that we cannot send young Americans off to put their lives in danger unless they have a clear understanding of why, and the complete support of the American people behind their mission.

Hershel W. Gober is a retired Army major who served two tours in Vietnam during the war. He received numerous decorations including the Soldier's Medal, Bronze Star, and the Purple Heart. He is Deputy Secretary of the U.S. Department of Veterans Affairs, and has led several Presidential delegations back to Vietnam during the 1990s to obtain the fullest possible accounting for America's missing military personnel.

BY ELIZABETH LOUISE KAHN

Piece of cake, I thought when Jan Scruggs asked me to respond to his question about what young people should know about Vietnam. I had been teaching this subject to undergraduates for many semesters. Nine years ago, Vietnam brought me and the thirty students in one of my classes so closely together that half of them were invited to my wedding—my marriage to a Vietnam veteran. Somehow though, I knew before I sat down to write this, that it wouldn't be easy.

First, I needed to reconnect with Vietnam on my own terms. Second, I needed to think of how to connect Vietnam to people now much younger than those students of the eighties and early nineties. So, I rented "Good Morning Vietnam" and watched it with my seven year-old son. Then, I reread the two anthologies that I co-edited—the first was produced out of the writings of my peers; the second was produced with my 1987 students. I found myself searching again for common ground between our generations. The common ground had been there intensely when we found ourselves in the same space—classroom, forum, gallery exhibition, writing and editing together. I was gratified with this initial preparation for at least 3 reasons: (1) I remembered all of the honesty of our teacher-student exchanges, and I re-experienced my own generational pain; (2) through all of its insane humor and good oldies music, "Good Morning Vietnam" is about the disgust for those who have the power to make war and the racism that fuels it; and (3) I think I found a way to answer Jan Scruggs' question.

Language, language, language—find your vocabulary, find a voice that can talk about Vietnam. There was an old, but well-used expression when I was in the anti-war movement in the late sixties: "Talk about the war." My veteran husband remembers his sister saying, "But what do I ask?" Soon after his return from Vietnam, Bill Ehrhart, a veteran poet, wrote a poem about this issue of intergenerational communication: The Teacher—". . . to find a voice that speaks the language that you speak." But of what vocabulary can our common language be made and what are the meanings we seek to construct? Now in 1996 and with the Vietnam War over twenty years away, that is the most important issue that we of different generations can address.

The students of my 1987 contemporary art history class produced an anthology of writings drawn from their responses to a two week forum on Vietnam and the arts. They entitled the first chapter "Lumps of Clay," a metaphor for their naïveté as they encountered the first round of visiting participants. These are the recurring words they used to describe this state of "innocence": fear, shock, remoteness, ignorance, helplessness. As the anthology proceeds, the vocabulary shifts from the less passive to the more active expressional meanings: compassion, resentment, frustration, sympathy, intensity, bombardment, entrapment. By the end of the anthology, a more future oriented choice of words emerge, most powerfully: understanding, self-evaluation, commitment. This was, as Incoming concludes, a journey.

In connection to a National Public Radio Satellite program on the Vietnam '87 forum, a colleague and I worked closely together and edited a retrospective anthology. The participants were asked to reflect on Vietnam a year after we had convened. Although the cynicism of the late sixties memories had not been erased by time and our collective 1987 endeavor, these writings rebounded in a positive way to the activism for which the student publication had argued. Together, the two anthologies represent a dialogue that diminishes the generational distance we all aimed to shorten. Here are some examples of the vocabulary used by the elders: wisdom, passion, honesty, critical thrust, trust, challenge, community, making a difference, responsibility. Reclaiming concludes with the question of legacy—the need to construct an intergenerational space in which all of those Vietnam era words can operate. Co-editor, Ellen Rocco, and I had made this clear on the dedication page: "For Joe and Willie, the next generation," who are our two young sons.

Blah, blah, blah. What good is talking or writing . . . or reading names on a black Wall? In a culture that can so easily neutralize and standardize the look, the feel, and the experiences of fear, shock, compassion, trust and difference, I think we need "to talk about the war" just as much, if not more, and record it. Although I am still a historian, veteran Jackson Day's poetry still reminds me of my professional flaws: ". . . You with your history books don't ask me how it was . . ."

Language again, those words and phrases spoken or written that stick with you. They are powerful, at the least, in their longevity. As I rethink Vietnam, two phrases come to mind again and again. After the 1987 forum as the Vietnam seminar semester concluded, I remember one student telling me, "We were like prisoners of war in that class." Another comes from a veteran friend who was there in 1987: "Just when you think Vietnam is no longer around, it comes up and pinches you." Call up one of the students who wrote for the anthology, and they'll know what those words mean.

Elizabeth Louise Kahn, associate professor, history of art, St. Lawrence University, Canton, New York, has been teaching about Vietnam in a variety of her courses. In addition to her radio and written work on the subject, she has delivered and organized a number of art-related conference papers and panels for the Vietnam area studies group of the Popular Culture Association of America.

BY ROD KANE

I fought in Vietnam as a teenager back in 1965. My tour lasted almost a year. What I remember of it, to this day, is the constant threat of ambushes and booby traps. It led to a high casualty rate and my job as a combat medic was to administer to the wounds of my men, pronouncing and logging the dead and the safe evacuation of both wounded and deceased.

This became a way of life—or death—depending on how one accepted it. I accepted it as a way of death as my days there turned to weeks and months, and as I lost more and more of my friends and replacements. My survival became bridled with futility and despair. Then, just as suddenly as it began, my tour was over and I was returned to the States.

Stunned.

Confused.

I was bitter and angry, as a cover for my grief and fear, at the loss involved in the war experience. Something from which the American society was very secure. In my rejection of the system and the anger I had towards it, I hurt myself. For awhile in my life, I let the war rule me. You can't allow destruction to rule your life.

Then, 15 years later in the early 1980s, when I was finally facing my grief and fear of the Vietnam experience, Jan Scruggs came forward with the proposition for a memorial to Vietnam veterans. At first, I was alarmed. Then, I felt the rush to promote as many memorials to the Vietnam veteran as possible. I was surprised at the amount of dissension amongst veterans over what a memorial should entail. But my real chagrin came about the day I passed by where the Memorial was being built. It was, at the time, nothing more than a big hole of fresh dirt. Holes like those I had seen as mass graves.

I was terrified at my recognition of the number of lives lost in that war. Of course, that terror was replaced by awe at the completion of the Memorial and its size. I could not go near it for years. Yet, in my mind, I knew where my dead fellows' names were in its chronology.

With the help of friends, which is what it takes, family and friends, I've come to face the Wall. Accept it. It's beautiful. Yet, it still reminds me of what has been true down through the decades, the centuries—it is easier to go off to war than it is to come back from one.

Rod Kane, U.S. paratrooper, combat medic, Vietnam veteran. Writer, author of Veterans Day (Orion 1990) (Pocketbooks 1991) and currently working on two books about post-Vietnam America.

BY STANLEY KARNOW

The same question arises in every discussion of the Vietnam experience: Could we have won the war? My answer is simple: The war was unwinnable.

The United States went into Southeast Asia with a huge arsenal—artillery, aircraft and the latest technological devices. At the height of the war, in late 1967, more than 500,000 American troops were involved. Our strategy was to break the will of the communists, and compel them to withdraw to North Vietnam—and we defeated them in every battle. But it was all futile.

What we did not understand was that we were up against an enemy willing to take unlimited losses. So, even though we killed them by the thousands, they would not surrender. It is estimated that at least one million communist soldiers died in the war. Compare Vietnam's population to ours, and it's as if we lost four million men. We believed that, with our overwhelming firepower, we could wear them down—but just the opposite occurred. By their tenacity and perseverance, they wore down the American public—so that, after years without progress, we felt that we had to withdraw.

General William C. Westmoreland, the U.S. commander, maintained that the communists accepted heavy casualties because Asians regard life as cheap. That comment showed a failure to understand the Vietnamese, their history and what makes them tick. They have been struggling against foreign invaders for 2,000 years—Chinese, Cambodians, French and Japanese. As a result, they became intensely nationalist—and would make extraordinary sacrifices to defend their homeland.

On a visit to Hanoi not long ago, I interviewed General Vo Ngyuen Giap, the commander of the communist forces. "How long were you prepared to go on fighting?" I asked him, to which he responded, "10, 20, 50, 100 years, as long as it took to win—regardless of cost." This willingness to accept such losses, incidentally, is not unique to the Vietnamese. Some 30,000 Americans—Union and Confederates—died in a single day in the battle of Antietam during our Civil War. They too were fighting for a cause.

The Vietnam War could have been avoided, in my view, if we had known more about the country. We would have realized that the Vietnamese communists were not part of some global communist machine but were basically nationalists. In that sense they were no threat to America's security. Only within the past 25 years have we recognized that communist movements in each country were different—and had different priorities. We paid a high tuition fee to learn that lesson: Nearly 60,000 names on the Vietnam Veterans Memorial in Washington.

Stanley Karnow covered the war in Vietnam from 1959 to the end. He is the author of Vietnam: A History, and winner of the Pulitzer Prize in History in 1990.

BY MICHAEL LEAVECK

Vietnam is still with us. It was a war that can be studied in history books and through numerous personal memoirs and recollections; a war that took 58,000 American lives and permanently disabled many thousands more. Thirty years ago, Vietnam was a country struggling to emerge from the frameworks of colonial rule and to establish a new identity as a nation. It is still a country now; a beautiful, lush, semi-tropical land nestled along the eastern rim of Southeast Asia. But it is a much different country, and is still struggling to define itself.

For Americans, who came of age during the 1960s, Vietnam was more than either a war or a country. It was a phenomenon, a defining event that simultaneously shaped and disrupted the culture and values of an entire generation. Perhaps, those of us who served in the war, especially those who were wounded or disabled, were more profoundly impacted. But the "generational" effects were not limited to the physical, combat, or geographical experience.

Just as the Great Depression defined the generation of the 1930s and the Civil War defined the generation of Walt Whitman and Mark Twain, my generation was forged in the crucible of Vietnam. Culturally, existentially and most of all politically, we are not the complacent, accepting and trusting demographic slice of the American populace that we would have been if Vietnam had not happened. For many of us, Vietnam is a crack in the lenses through which we see the world. We have been deemed less patriotic, but that is only true if a narrow and simplistic definition of patriotism is accepted.

It changed permanently the way we regard many of the institutions in American society. The military, the news media, the U.S. Congress, and the Presidency are all viewed differently and with more mistrust by the generation which is now nearing fifty than from the way those same sectors of society were looked upon by those in the generation preceding us. Likewise, churches, civic organizations, schools, and local governments have all been treated and engaged with more reservation and less commitment by the Vietnam-era alumni.

American institutions themselves changed in response to the transformation in values and orientation, and mostly for the better. We no longer "go it alone" in our foreign policy, and we are much more reluctant to use our military as an international police force. Our legislative bodies and the attendant political processes are much more open to involvement by ordinary citizens. The news media no longer give those in power, or those aspiring to it, a free ride.

It is true that Watergate, television, and the excesses of the sixties helped to shape the attitudes and values of the baby-boomers in the same direction. It must be remembered, however, that the crimes of the Nixon Administration began as a reaction to the anti-Vietnam War movement. Many of the sixties cultural phenomena were at least purported to be a reaction to the Vietnam War, and for the first time, television had brought the war into our living rooms. Every night at dinner time, we were confronted with body counts and images of destruction.

The decline of trust in each other, in our institutions, and in ourselves, which began its long cascading tumble during the Vietnam War, probably bottomed-out at long last, just a few short years ago. It remains to be seen, however, if we can recapture, as a people and not just for our generation, the kind of optimism and American "can do" attitude recently portrayed in the movie "Apollo Thirteen."

Just as Vietnam cannot be seen as the mono-causal element in America's jaundice of faith and hope, there is no magic talisman to heal us all and make us whole. But there are starting points and catalysts for healing: the Vietnam Veterans Memorial is one of the more useful and powerful of such catalysts. Those whose names are engraved on the Vietnam Veterans Memorial fought and died out of pure and idealistic motivations. Whatever misadventure the war itself might have been, and whatever sadness and anger seeps into one's consciousness at the Memorial because of the tragedy of Vietnam, that goodness and idealism must be remembered too. We should also remember the tremendous outpouring of support and contributions from the American people that made the Memorial possible. "We were soldiers once, and young" quotes a verse, and we were idealistic and trusting, too. Perhaps, we can be again.

Michael Leaveck is a Navy Vietnam veteran who served aboard the USS Turner Joy in 1965 and 1966. He has been involved in advocating on behalf of, and providing services to, Vietnam veterans and their families in various capacities since 1968. He is currently the Deputy Director of a program set up to distribute funds from the Agent Orange Class Action Lawsuit.

BY MARC LEEPSON

If I had to pick one issue for high school students to understand about the American war in Vietnam, it would be the lack of understanding among individual Americans and our national leaders about Vietnam's history, culture and society. Perhaps I can best convey that idea by explaining what was going on in my mind when I got drafted and was sent to Vietnam.

I got drafted into the Army on July 11, 1967. I was twenty-two and had just graduated from college. But I didn't know very much about what was happening in Vietnam. I knew there was a war going on. And I knew that the draft had caught up to me after a failed attempt to get into Air Force officer's training school.

I went in the Army willingly, knowing that I would more than likely be sent to Vietnam. I was nervous about going to the war zone, but I figured that if my country was involved, the cause was just.

I soon learned otherwise. My feeling that I was serving my country in a good cause vanished within weeks after I landed in Vietnam on December 13, 1967. By that time, I'd seen firsthand and learned from others that the massive American troop commitment seemed to be the only thing keeping the Communists from taking over South Vietnam. I also came to see that the South Vietnamese Army—our ally—seemed to be riddled with corruption and incompetence, as was the South Vietnamese government.

I didn't know one GI in Vietnam who was a zealous anti-communist. Just about every one of us merely wanted to put in our time and get home alive. I was lucky and did just that. But today, I'm not certain if I did the right thing by going to Vietnam. I did nothing I'm ashamed of. But I didn't have to go, and I took part in a war that probably should not have been fought.

High school students should put themselves in my shoes back in 1967. When the draft was breathing down my neck,

I decided to do what I thought was my duty. But I didn't know what I was getting myself into. Perhaps if I had more knowledge about Vietnam, I would have chosen a different path.

Our country, as a whole, didn't know what it was getting into in Vietnam, and that's the main reason the war became a disaster. That's the most important thing, I believe, for students to understand about that war. We went into Vietnam with little knowledge of Vietnamese history, society, or culture—or of the geopolitical situation in Southeast Asia.

We may have gone in for the best of reasons—to help a non-communist country stave off communism—but we botched things terribly. Perhaps if the presidents, generals, foreign affairs experts, national security advisers and American citizens in general had known more about Vietnam, Southeast Asian politics, and international communism, the United Sates never would have sent troops to Vietnam.

Marc Leepson served with the 527 Personnel Services Co. in Qui Nhon, South Vietnam, from December 1967 to December 1968. A free-lance writer, he is arts editor and columnist for The VVA Veteran, *the newspaper published by Vietnam Veterans Of America in Washington, D.C.*

BY VIOLET C. LONG

My first visit to the Vietnam Veterans Memorial was in the summer of 1986. I must admit, I went there very reluctantly. Although I had been a member of the American Gold Star Mothers, Inc. since 1971 and felt comfortable sharing that common bond with the Mothers in our local chapter, I still harbored much bitterness for the loss of our son in Vietnam. I said goodbye to him in January 1969. He was returned to us eight months later in a closed casket. The "unknown" element has always been difficult for me to accept.

What was my first impression of the Wall? I found the number of names engraved on it overwhelming. Each name represented: a human being—sons, daughters, brothers, sisters, husbands; and many different cultures. But I also became aware that there was one thing they had in common—each one had a mother and father. In this, I found comfort. I was no longer alone in my grief.

From 1988 to 1993, I was privileged to be a member on the National Board of the American Gold Star Mothers and visited the Wall every time I was in D.C. I especially looked forward to Gold Star Mothers Day the last Sunday in September of each year. Early Sunday morning, the Board members would go to the Wall to place a United States flag at each panel for our special day. After the service in Arlington National Cemetery, we returned to the Memorial to place our Gold Star wreath. Mothers always lingered there—it was difficult to leave and return to National Headquarters. The year I was National President, I received a special request from a Mother in Illinois when a member of our Board passed away. At the time of her funeral, I was asked to go the Memorial and place a yellow rose and an American flag at the panel where her son's name was engraved.

My visits to the Memorial now are truly times for personal reflection—because memories are the immeasurable history of our past. I want to share some of my personal reflections with you.

Active in the Youth Department of our local church, my husband and I had taken a young couple on a retreat on the first weekend in September 1969. The weather was beautiful, the leaves were beginning to color, and it was a wonderful weekend in God's world. When we returned home, there were two military servicemen. They had been waiting all day for us to break the news of Charles' death. The family circle was broken, never to be the same. Charles, our son, was laid to rest the day he was to leave Vietnam for his R&R in Australia. He was a "homebody" and never liked to travel too far from home. Knowing this, a friend of mine wrote a poem for me with these closing lines, which will always be treasured:

Ironic, that he who never chose to roam,
should leave so young, should die so far from home.

I have always had a special interest in our young people, and would like to encourage them, particularly high school students, to visit the Memorial. A visit to the Memorial has a different meaning for each of us. But one quickly realizes that *Freedom is Not Free*. We need to honor and remember the human sacrifice that is made when our citizens are asked to serve their country. While serving in the Armed Forces is the most selfless act anyone could perform for their country, it is not the only way to answer to our country's call. An outstanding example of this was the 1996 blizzard and flood in Pennsylvania, my home state. Young people and children rallied to the cause valiantly by collecting clothing, shoes, blankets, food, and money in more ways than can be described here. America's forecast is not as bleak as some may think. We can all be a part of the solution by the giving of ourselves.

The following lines could well be spoken by any one of the loved ones whose name is forever engraved on the Memorial, and always in our hearts:

When you're lonely and sick at heart,
Go to the friends we know,
And bury your sorrows in doing good deeds,
MISS ME . . . But let me go.

— Author Unknown

Violet C. Long is the Department and Chapter Officer and the Past National President of the American Gold Star Mothers, Inc. She is also the Editor of The Gold Star Mothers Newsletter.

BY GEORGE MCGOVERN

The Vietnam War was fought by some of the bravest soldiers ever to go into battle. This was true of both the American soldier and the Vietnamese, who opposed them. As a combat pilot in World War II, I fought with comrades who were both dedicated and skillful. The American soldiers I visited in Vietnam were equally courageous and skillful.

Why then did we fail to achieve our objectives in Vietnam? Why did so many patriotic Americans—both civilian and military—come to believe that American participation was a mistake? Why did I oppose the war and seek the Presidency on a pledge to end it?

I opposed the war because I believed that our policy makers were wrong in ordering our military forces to fight in Vietnam. Those policy makers said that we had to go into Vietnam to oppose communism. It was believed that the Vietnamese leader, Ho Chi Minh, a communist, was simply a stooge of Communist Russia and China.

To be sure, Ho was a communist. But he was even more fundamentally a Vietnamese patriot who had successfully led the revolution of his people against their French colonial masters. In that sense, he was seen by most of the Vietnamese people as being like George Washington, who two centuries earlier had led an American revolution against British colonialists. President Eisenhower estimated that, in an honest election, Ho would have won eighty percent of the vote in both the North and the South of Vietnam.

Unfortunately, our policy makers turned their backs on this political reality and ignored the history of Vietnam. They encouraged the creation of a regime in the South that had few, if any, credentials other than its willingness to wave an anti-communist banner. That regime largely ignored the needs of the people and permitted a high level of corruption and misrule. Many of its officials and supporters had collaborated with the French, instead of supporting the Vietnamese struggle for independence led by Ho Chi Minh. The various regimes our policy makers supported in South Vietnam were not worthy of either Vietnamese or American support.

Ho Chi Minh did get arms and other aid from Russia and China. But he was never controlled by any outside power.

Former Secretary of Defense, Robert McNamara—a chief architect of the Vietnam War policy—has now concluded that his policy was "a terrible mistake." That was my view more than 30 years ago. It remains my view today. Never again should we commit our soldiers abroad without first knowing what the political, military, cultural, and historical realities are in the proposed area of combat. We owe our soldiers and our nation this precaution.

George McGovern, former U.S. Senator and 1972 Presidential Nominee, is currently President of the Middle East Policy Council and Honorary Chair for the National Council on Alcoholism and Drug Dependence (NCADD).

BY JOHN MCNEILL

It was a simple event and when it occurred, I had no indication it would become an image forever etched in my mind. We were convoying an artillery battery of 175 millimeter guns along a river valley when, out of the corner of my eye, I noticed a group of Montagnard children playing outside their village. One fell down and obviously began crying for his mother; nothing more seemingly out of the ordinary than that.

But it marked a turn-around in my thinking about the war. Up until that time, the images of Vietnam were of a very poor, rodent-infested, cholera-ridden, agrarian land where people seemed alien—the epitome of a peasant society. It was a place with which I desired no association. At that moment, however, a basic humanity was demonstrated by the obvious: Vietnamese children cried when hurt, and mothers took care of those injuries. With this attitude transformation, the beauty of the country also became more readily apparent: the old French colonial rubber plantations, the dense green mountains, the white sand beaches, and Saigon, which was well deserving of its title "the Paris of the Orient."

It is important to note that the war had progressed so favorably, at that time (mid-1969), that these Montagnard children could venture safely out of their unusually well-fortified camps. Tactically, the North Vietnamese and the Viet Cong were being soundly beaten. By the end of the Cambodian excursion the next year, they essentially ceased to exist as a substantial military force. But the resolve to endure in their attempt to unify Vietnam, while arguably sorely stretched, had not been broken, and the Soviet Union's commitment of resources to their ally was not deterred. As we well know from history, that level of commitment was not the same for the United States.

Our lack of commitment led, eventually, to increased devastation. The United States ultimately lost approximately

58,000 killed; the Vietnamese casualties were supposedly in the millions. That was a telling portrait of Vietnam. The war did not generate the excitement of the movie "Rambo." Indeed, Hollywood has rarely been able to capture the proper perspective, showing far more imagination than fact. (None more so than in "The Deer Hunter," the 1978 Academy Award for Best Picture, which Leonard Maltin described as a "sensitive, painful, evocative work . . .") The one poignant movie for me is "The Killing Fields." The documented indiscriminate massacre of an estimated three million Cambodians by the communists is an all too graphic symbolism on the eventual result of the war.

I wonder often what has become of the Vietnamese and Cambodians that I came to like and admire once they were stripped of the protection provided by the United States. It seems evident that they have suffered greatly after our ignominious evacuation and the subsequent unmitigated ruthlessness of the communists in consolidating their power. Because of their close association with the Special Forces, the Montagnards were very susceptible; it is highly unlikely that those playing children remained alive for very long after the communist victory. Accordingly, our lack of sustained commitment to those people is an ever-lasting guilt.

It is often stated that time is a great healer and that may prove to be true in Vietnam. Ironically, the people who suffered under the communist tyranny now will have the most to gain with the correct decision to reestablish diplomatic relations. The communist hard-liners are rapidly "dying out" and it is only a matter of time that the kind of democracy we once envisioned for the South Vietnamese and Cambodians will be a reality. What we didn't have the fortitude to do tactically and strategically over 20 years ago, will now likely occur as a result of diplomacy—the factor that was previously thought, and naively relied on, to be the original solution in 1973.

John McNeill is currently employed by the Veterans of Foreign Wars of the United States providing pro bono service to veterans. He served in the Republic of Vietnam from March 1969 to 1970 as a field artillery forward observer, air observer, and battery executive officer.

BY LARRY MCQUILLAN

When people think about the Vietnam War, many think about the passions and controversy it generated at home and the television images of protesters confronting riot police. My images are different. I think of the Americans who served there, many of them just out of high school. Some are among the more than 58,000 names on "the Wall." Some came back permanently disabled. All came back different, changed by the intensity of war.

Most Vietnam veterans don't talk about the war very much, but that doesn't mean their experiences should be ignored. The sacrifices that were made deserve to be remembered. The lessons that were learned must never be forgotten.

There really are two closely-related lessons that resulted from America's experience in Vietnam. First, all of us should be open-minded when it comes to questioning what our government is doing. Being a "good American" means asking questions. The second lesson is that young people can make a difference. They were the ones who first started to question whether we should be in Vietnam. Eventually, they forced the rest of the country to start asking questions, as well.

Back in 1959, when the first U.S. servicemen were killed in Vietnam, most Americans assumed the government in Washington knew what it was doing. That attitude continued until the 1968 Tet Offensive by the North Vietnamese Army and the Viet Cong began to generate doubts about the war. Young people started raising questions about America's policies and their costs—eventually, leading their elders to do the same. Finally, in 1973, most of the U.S. forces were withdrawn from Vietnam.

As someone who served in the Army and hitched rides on helicopters to cover the war for Pacific Stars & Stripes, the "hometown" paper for the troops in Vietnam, I have mixed emotions about the war. I have no doubts, however, about the horrors that nearly two million Americans were exposed to there. That's why it makes me angry to hear Robert McNamara, who for seven years was Secretary of Defense, now say that he had private doubts about the war and the "misjudgments" that were made in our policy.

The memories of Vietnam never really leave me, and I don't want them to because they have created a responsibility. Now that I am a journalist in Washington, I find those memories prompting me to ask the government officials "Why?" to make sure that they can defend the positions they advocate. It is a responsibility that I feel I have to those who served in Vietnam and for the young men and women now asked to serve in Bosnia or on any other military mission.

The lessons of Vietnam are a responsibility for all of us. It was high school and college-age Americans who first asked the tough questions concerning Vietnam. Unsatisfied with the answers they received, they made a difference. No one changes the world by themselves, and no one changes the world by assuming it can't be done.

We should never be cynical and assume the government is wrong, but we have a right to be convinced that its policies are correct. We just have to ask the question "Why?"

Larry McQuillan, who was a Spec. 4 in the Army, covered the war in Vietnam for Pacific Stars & Stripes. Currently, he is a White House correspondent for Reuters News Service.

BY JAMES MEEK

In March, 1965, as U.S. Marines made an uneventful, but significant, amphibious landing on the picturesque beaches of Da Nang, Republic of Vietnam, there already were protests back home against just such a buildup of American forces involved in yet another Asian war. And these demonstrations were getting louder and more defiant.

In 1965, the war-peace chasm that started to divide the people of the United States forced change—change which mimicked the numbing emotions felt after our own catastrophic War Between the States one hundred years before.

In the chaotic '60s, Vietnam became the rock and roll war. The music came from machine guns raging full-on and the talent arrived in green fatigues, followed for the first time by television news cameras. It was our gringo pop culture run amok, and Vietnam soon resembled the blast point of a long forgotten, and bombed-into-submission, American suburb.

Those who did not go to Vietnam could never understand those who did. To many Americans, the war was about a handful of policy makers in Washington, DC, who felt the U.S. commitment there was an essential stand against Communism's encroachment. They could see no sense in spending the lives of our young people and our tax dollars on a military conflict thousands of miles and a million light years away.

Those who did go to Vietnam could never understand those who did not. Coming back was like coming down and pain was an envelope they pushed alone, struggling to re-adjust from the physical hazards of the combat zone to the social peril of a society that rejected them.

The years passed. Vietnam veterans aching to tell their painful stories silenced themselves when they realized nobody wanted to listen. People at home had all heard enough.

They had heard the shouting and the shooting at marches against the war. They had listened to the politicians and the pundits, and they had watched in horror as the body count grew into the thousands on their TV sets. They had argued with family, they had argued with friends. They had watched so many leave, they protected those left behind. They missed the ones who didn't come back. And now, finally, they wanted to put that word—"Vietnam"—that awful, corrupt, seething word into the dark corners of the past.

In November, 1982, the Vietnam Veterans Memorial was dedicated in Washington, DC, amid much controversy and biting criticism. It was called "a black gash of shame" by some, and other critics said it would be the site of future anti-war demonstrations. It seemed like the heart-wrenching divisions caused by the war in Vietnam would pierce even deeper into our national spirit.

Then something unexpected happened: Americans began to change. The new Memorial forced divisions over the war out into the open. It inspired dialogue, and even heated discussions gave relief. Because of the Memorial, people were talking about Vietnam again and it helped to heal the divisiveness.

But by then, many Vietnam veterans didn't want to talk about it.

The enemy in Vietnam, the ghostly and elusive Viet Cong, had tapped into the most effective weapon of war—the human imagination. This is where fear lives. Now, only seven years after the war ended in 1975, fear once again engulfed the imagination of those who fought in it.

Just as the country seemed to be reexamining the long "Television War," which Vietnam was appropriately nick-named, veterans feared a reprisal of the hatred so many of their fellow Americans had directed at them for serving there. Some veterans, who had years before given up any hope of making people understand the terror and horror of this war, believed it pointless to try, even as the country celebrated their sacrifice and finally began to welcome them home.

Today, the hope for Vietnam veterans rests in the generation which followed them, the children of the Vietnam era.

Young Americans want to know about the Vietnam War. They want to learn about it from those who survived it. They want to understand the frustration and anguish of the men and women who served and fought and returned to face the adversity of a nation which turned its back on them. They want to see the human dimension of the war more than the political dimension.

Most importantly, young people are willing to listen. In the telling of their stories, the Vietnam veteran can heal the wounds of a divided nation by helping us to finally understand.

James Gordon Meek, 26, is the politics editor for the first magazine on CD ROM, and was the first "interactive correspondent" to receive credentials from the U.S. Capitol news galleries. He has volunteered and worked for the VVMF since 1983, and has spent much time at the Wall listening to the stories of Vietnam veterans.

BY SHAD MESHAD

The Vietnam War caused a division in this country like no other war. While there were many in favor of the United States' intervention in Vietnam, many were opposed to any involvement whatsoever. While the political and armed forces scaled up the war during the 1960s, many people in the country who opposed the war staged massive demonstrations and attempted to influence the government to end the war.

One of the reasons it was so difficult for civilians to begin to understand the problems plaguing this unpopular war was the inability to separate the war from the warriors. For the first time, Americans experienced the tragedy and the brutality of war televised in their living rooms after dinner. The public was forced to come face to face with combat. Media coverage put the combat servicemen in the spotlight, portraying them as perpetrators of death and destruction, unlike the noble heroes of past wars. The Vietnam servicemen and women, like all who had served before them, risked their lives on a daily and hourly basis to ensure freedom for those who waited at home. Yet, the Vietnam veteran came home to criticism and blame for being part of this vastly unpopular war, through no fault of their own. America was not ready to accept the tragedy of war. Our country somehow believed that this war was more cruel than others. Almost by default, Vietnam veterans became the target at which the public could vent its frustration about this unpopular "political" action.

What we need to understand is that there are no winners in any war, including the Vietnam War. While war is continually portrayed in movies and books, there is no way to accurately depict the reality and the brutality of the battlefield. Movies fail to prepare the viewer for the death of a fellow soldier, nor do they convey the effect of being an unwilling participant in the killing of an enemy. The most traumatic impact for a soldier is that moment when he loses his innocence during the encounter with the enemy. A soldier must rely not only on training, but also on luck to survive. Only those who have experienced the profound circumstances of battle can understand the high level of anxiety, and the trauma, resulting from combat.

Winning offers little solace to those who have the war experience. Death occurs on all sides, and even a victor changes dramatically, becoming impoverished in his or her mental, physical, and spiritual life. One who has not lived such a trauma must remain appreciative of the significance of these sensational transformations to the human psyche. No one involved in these life and death encounters is left unscathed. Thousands of Vietnam combat veterans manifest haunting memories which result in periodic feelings of anxiety, and lifelong inability to cope with a rational society.

Wars have been glamorized in poetry, novels, and songs and dramatized to attract the interest of the audience, but these forms fail to adequately create an understanding of the actual events soldiers experience day to day. War cannot be simplified into a series of isolated acts.

It is important to understand the contradictory nature of war. Those who have lived, and continue to live the effects of combat, who touch upon the terrible loss of life and the tragic consequences of the soldiers who came home, and those who didn't, are a reminder of the tragedy of war. I believe the best way to understand the Vietnam War is to pay attention to those authors who have been there. There is very little information available in high school history books. We can read about the dates, the numbers of troops, perhaps, and some of the famous battles—the Tet Offensive, Hamburger Hill—the Hanoi Hilton, and other events. But these writings tend to portray the Vietnam War in an antiseptic manner. Over the past twenty years, there has been a tremendous outpouring of literature, books, stories, and poetry about the Vietnam War. To truly understand the Vietnam experience, one can begin by reading the body of literature written by actual combat veterans.

Vietnam veterans suffered much condemnation from the country they loved, the country for whom they offered to die. Soldiers in Vietnam read about the protests, the riots, and the continual damnation from home, and wondered who the real enemy was. To this day, many of these heroes cannot function in society. They feel ostracized by our people, and by a government which failed to adequately support them when they returned to our shores.

There are no winners in war. You cannot make war go away by denying it as a part of our country's history. If you look around our city streets, you will find that many of today's homeless population are the remnants of a force of combat veterans, who feel that they have no country. The reality of war is clear and permanent for those who have experienced it. The best lesson one can learn from any war is that there are no real winners, at least not for those who have to fight it.

Shad Meshad, a Captain in the U.S. Army, served one tour in Vietnam as a mental health officer for I and II Corps. He returned to start the Vietnam Veterans Resocializing Unit at the Brentwood VA Hospital in 1971, and in 1979 pioneered the nationwide Vietnam Vet Center Outreach Program. In 1985, he founded the Vietnam Veterans Aid Foundation (now known as the National Veterans Foundation due to expanded services to include all veterans), which presently serves over 150,000 veterans and dependents each year.

BY JANICE A. NARK

On Veterans Day 1994, I participated in a panel discussion at a local community college. Four soldiers and I, the nurse—all Vietnam vets—came to tell our stories. The audience was as diverse in their occupations as in their ages, which spanned about seven decades. As diverse as, I suppose, their reasons for coming to hear us speak, to learn about Vietnam.

I still hadn't gotten over the notion of people wanting to know about the war, since for almost 20 years no one asked, and I certainly didn't tell. But here we were and each in turn shared our stories, some for the first time. This was not a rehearsed group and there was a lot of emotion and spontaneous tears; stories of bravery and cowardice, of anger and fear, and enduring sadness.

I spoke briefly of my tour of duty, my years of silence, and about the Wall and how it helped me come to peace with my memories. At the conclusion of the discussion, a teenage girl came up to me and said, "When I went to the Wall, I was just overwhelmed. I cried and cried, and I don't know why—I have no right."

I have no right. How many times I've thought that, heard it, read it, said it! *I'm alive, they're dead . . . I couldn't get to him . . . if only . . . I didn't suffer . . . I didn't do enough . . . I had to do it . . . I wasn't old enough to go . . . I protested the war.*

"I have no right," she said, in essence, I'm not entitled to these feelings. Ah, the post-war guilt reaches out to those who hadn't even been born yet. I smiled into those young eyes, and there was so much I wanted to say. "Of course, you have the right. The Vietnam Veterans Memorial is an extraordinarily powerful monument. It's physically powerful. Walking the length of all those names inscribed in granite, that carry you down into the earth and back again. It is a physical journey that touches every fiber of your body. It's psychologically powerful. Emotions are readily transferable from person to person. You were experiencing all the feelings that were present: The pain, grief, anger, sadness and despair of the men and women who served, of those who didn't, of those who loved, of those who lost, of the ones who lived, and of the ones who died; all the emotions of those who have questions still unanswered, and of those to whom the truth is all too evident. It is a healing ground for those who have come together there. It is a respite from the real world for those who are forever torn apart. Understand that you cried for all of them because you felt their pain. You are a daughter of America. I pray your generation will find a path towards peace instead of war. I hope you never have to know personally what the Wall represents to the millions of Americans who lived its mission."

I wanted to say all that and so much more. But all I think I could manage was to touch her arm and say, "It's a very emotional place, and you have every right to cry."

Janice A. Nark served as a nurse in Vietnam in 1970–71. She is now a certified ski instructor, entrepreneur and motivational speaker whose sense of humor has sustained her and continues to carry audiences along on enlightening, educational and entertaining journeys.

BY ERIKA NIEDOWSKI

Although it's sometimes called "the forgotten war," Vietnam is probably the most remembered war in American history. There, in the jungles and rice paddies more than 9,000 miles away, America lost what it had cherished the most: its innocence. And for the first time, its past became a burden, rather than a source of pride.

The 10,000 day war—the longest war in American history—left more than 58,000 names inscribed on the Vietnam Veterans Memorial in Washington, and it cost over $150 billion.

President Lyndon Johnson lied to us about the war's escalation and our ability to win it. He watched his dream of a Great Society die in the process. Protesters, calling American soldiers "baby killers," clashed with police and National Guardsmen in the streets and on college campuses. After one such incident at Ohio's Kent State University, four students lay dead. And after the 1968 battle for Bien Hoa, a town outside of Siagon, an Army major made sense of the waste before him declaring, "We had to destroy the village in order to save it." By the end of the 1960s, America's goal in Vietnam was not to safeguard freedom or promote democracy, but to avoid a humiliating defeat. President Nixon spoke not of peace, but of "peace with honor."

In the most fundamental way, of course, Vietnam was no different from any other war. Times and technologies change, but the realities of war—from villages burned to soldiers sent home in body bags—stay the same. In the American mind, though, Vietnam was the antithesis of previous wars. Unlike World War II, remembered as the "Good War," there were no heroic images of John Wayne, no raising of the flag at Iwo Jima. There wasn't any Adolf Hitler or Pearl Harbor to galvanize the country. There wasn't any homecoming celebration or sense of closure. Mostly, there was bitterness.

If this country's hands had been tied during the war, afterwards they were dirty. Vietnam dealt us a military defeat—

although, this is being disputed. But it was a symbolic defeat that lingered. Militarily, we learned about the limitations of our "superior" high-technology equipment and the near impossibility of winning a war in which we weren't sure if the enemy was the Viet Cong, the jungle heat, or the very people we were trying to "save." More disturbing was how the war had turned us against each other, and how fallible we realized our government could be. After the war, the United States was no longer the city upon a hill that it so prided itself in being.

Vietnam had become a lens through which we clarify our culture and test our values. It is still with us, even 20 years after the last helicopter lifted off from Saigon. The war didn't create, but rather illuminated, our flaws. And for that reason, we want to forget about the Vietnam War—but can't.

Erika Niedowski writes for The Hill newspaper in Washington, D.C. She wrote her undergraduate thesis, "War, Myth and Memory: Writing Vietnam into History," at Georgetown University on the Vietnam War, as portrayed in fiction and nonfiction.

BY TERRENCE O'DONNELL

In March 1969, when I boarded an aircraft at Travis Air Force Base en route to South Vietnam, I hadn't given much thought to the legitimacy, efficacy and long-term implications of the U.S. commitment to that embattled, war torn nation. I had grown up in a military family, graduated from the U.S. Air Force Academy, and had learned well the importance of the chain of command and the need for strict obedience to military orders. Thus, once I received my orders, I simply began packing—no questions, no debate, no doubts, no reluctance, no second guessing and certainly no "geopolitical analysis." I had my orders and I was on my way. That's what I had been taught, and at the time, that's all that mattered.

My year-long tour of duty in-country passed relatively uneventfully. A few random 122mm rockets dropped near my quarters but not close enough to do any damage. A few shots were fired at my jeep outside DaNang and at my helicopter near Phu Cat, but all of this seemed impersonal and none of it impressed me as particularly significant. I worked hard, counted the days, visited Hong Kong on "R&R," complained about the food and heat, received a couple of awards, packed my bags and said farewell to Vietnam and the friends who remained behind. I was lucky—no one in my unit was killed or seriously wounded, and I was spared the horrible and tragic experiences suffered by so many of our colleagues in arms. I was happy to return to the United States and my family, and had absolutely no interest in volunteering for a second tour. I was proud that I had served and had no sympathy for those who illegally dodged the call—and that has not changed.

Only after I returned home did the tough questions start to run through my mind, like the flow of a never ending river—day in and day out. Why were we really there? What did we hope to accomplish? How could we ever succeed if we insisted on fighting according to their rules, rather than ours?

How many lives would we pour into this bottomless pit of conflict? Would we change the phony self-imposed limitations on the way hostilities were conducted? Why don't we "take the gloves off" or get out? What about the strife in the streets and the turmoil on the campuses? Did my tour of duty make a difference—did it count for something? And most of all, what about the casualties: the KIAs, the MIAs and their loved ones? What about the misery and torment spewing from this seemingly endless conflict? And what about the helicopter medical evacuation zone near South Vietnam quarters that never ceased delivering the wounded and the dead to the hospital and the morgue? I didn't have any good answers, but I could not stop asking. It didn't seem that anyone had good answers—our Commanders-In-Chief—Kennedy, Johnson, Nixon or Ford—the Congress, the Pentagon, the State Department, the news media, the veterans, the campuses, the hawks or the doves. We seemed mired in a tragic debacle—a grinding maze of death that was bereft of any suitable avenue of escape.

There was plenty of blame to go around but, from my perspective, no valid purpose for assessing it except to learn crucial lessons in order to save future generations from the dictate that history is destined to repeat itself. Vietnam is one chapter that must not be repeated. And that is where the Vietnam Veterans Memorial comes in. True, it is a powerful tribute to duty, honor, and country—to dedication, service, patriotism and ultimate sacrifice. But, perhaps even more compelling, it is a stark beacon in the night, a bright line, a guiding star forever warning our nation's leadership to steer clear of ill-advised international undertakings, and to commit our armed forces only when there are clear objectives, national support, and the means to reasonably defend our troops. The Memorial calls out to all who will listen: "Reflect. Think before acting and never, never put American fighting men and women in harm's way without giving them the tools, leeway and support to do the job, and do it right—no more artificial rules of engagement that hobble our warriors and lead to a bloody stalemate. By all means, fight when necessary, fight to protect our true national interests, but fight to win."

At the Memorial, the walkway to the apex is easy to traverse. You can feel momentum build as you walk down this hallowed path drawn by what lies ahead, determined to reach the bottom and see it all. But before you build up too much speed, like a wagon rolling down an incline, before you go too far, pause and study the names. Like Vietnam, the number of casualties are few at first, but with each panel, the number increases. The names compel the visitor to stop. Through the names, the Memorial speaks to us. Its message is both simple and profound: "Look deeply into my black granite face and see yourself in the reflection—your face, super-imposed on the names. Never forget the names, the names, the names for they hold the answer."

Terrence O'Donnell served in Vietnam with U.S. Air Force Special Investigations as a Counter Intelligence Officer. He is an attorney, and was General Counsel to the Department of Defense under President Bush. He is now a partner with the firm of Williams and Connolly.

BY PETER C. ROLLINS

A dimension of the Vietnam conflict too often overlooked is the impact of media on America's perceptions of the war—at the time and later. We live with the resulting distortions and veterans suffer as a result.

During the war, news stories flashed back to the nation's living rooms with instant analysis of events which reporters may not have fully understood. The Tet Offensive, in 1968, is the most dramatic case in point. Not long after the successful offensive, Don Oberdorfer of the Washington Post wrote an insightful book entitled, Tet (New York: Doubleday, 1971). The seasoned reporter criticized the print and visual media for mis-reporting an allied victory—i.e., a victory for our South Vietnamese friends and for the U.S. forces—as a defeat.

Some four years later, Peter Braestrup, the top reporter for the Washington Post during the Tet Offensive, produced a two-volume work entitled Tet: How the American Press and Television Reported and Interpreted the Crisis of Tet 1968 . . . (Yale University Press, 1976). Both Oberdorfer and Braestrup concluded that the drive for exciting visual stories, plus the demand for instant analysis clouded the judgment of reporters and led to serious misrepresentation of the Vietnam conflict back in the United States.

In the mid-1980s, my research led me to similar conclusions about television and Vietnam. In an article for the Journal of American Culture (4 [1981]:114-135), I outlined my critique. Later, I made two television programs about press bias during the Vietnam War, both narrated by Charlton Heston: "Television's Vietnam: The Impact of Media" and "Television's Vietnam: The Real Story" (Sony Video). Both illustrate the bad reporting with film clips—which are then critiqued by diplomats, experts on the press, and by U.S. fighting men who lived through the battles that were so badly represented on America's television screens.

After the war, films such as "Apocalypse Now," "Platoon,"

and the "Rambo" series projected Vietnam images on the movie screen. Some veterans have praised these films, but—as with television—I have tried to point out the inaccuracies and distortions of these media portrayals. For a veteran's perspective of the Vietnam films, read Vietnam at the Movies by Michael Lee Lanning (New York: Fawcett-Columbine, 1994). My own comments on the errors of Hollywood are in an article entitled "Using Popular Culture to Study the Vietnam War: Perils and Possibilities" in Popular Culture in the United States, ed. Peter Freese (Essen: Die Blau Eule, 1994: 221-31).

Ninety-nine percent of American soldiers, sailors, and marines behaved in a moral and legal fashion in Vietnam. You would not know that from television or from Hollywood films. Students need to ponder this paradox and to apply the results of their thinking to visual reporting today.

Dr. Peter C. Rollins served in Vietnam as a rifle and weapons platoon commander in the U.S. Marines—operating in the DaNang and Chu Lai areas during 1965. Today, he is a Regents Professor of English at Oklahoma State University, and Vice President of the Vietnam Veterans Institute.

BY MARY B. SCHAAF

The most important issue for high school students, as well as all American citizens, to understand about the Vietnam War is that it officially ended January 27, 1973 for the United States—the cease fire agreement was signed in Paris. But the war devastated and changed the destiny of so many lives that even today, personal battles continue to be fought.

Severely wounded on September 5, 1969, he lived for twenty-one years with a bullet lodged in his heart, the other slug carried around his neck on a silver chain, and shrapnel embedded in his leg and back; walked on Canadian crutches (attached to the forearms) with the help of leg braces; and coped with severe pain. These were all parts of the Vietnam legacy for my husband, Lee R. Schaaf. The main attributes that disabled veterans exhibit every day of their lives are tremendous sacrifice, courage, determination, and a continuous striving for self-preservation. All of these are necessary to help attain various degrees of normalcy in the American dream. Their ongoing and lifelong rehabilitation, heroism, and hope for the future are important elements in overcoming great odds in attempting to come back and succeed. For some, just being alive is a success story.

Fifty eight thousand soldiers died in Vietnam, but nearly 304,000 more were wounded. In this war, the means of warfare became more deadly and virulent than in previous wars. Weapons were often geared to maim, rather than kill, as seen with the booby traps and claymore mines filled with garbage and bacteria-infested shrapnel meant to cause serious, long-lasting infections. And they did.

To these veterans, disabled physically and mentally, the Vietnam experience remains part of their ongoing life experiences. History has shown that as memories of the war fade, the problems of the veterans tend to be minimized or forgotten as well.

The bureaucracy has made it even more difficult to be a disabled veteran. Many cannot work steadily or at all because of their injuries. It is discouraging to realize that veterans' groups are constantly battling to keep the government from slashing disability percentages and ultimately decreasing the benefits and care that veterans should be entitled to.

Disabled, handicapped veterans have special needs. The young people of today and tomorrow need to be keenly aware that they can make a difference in these people's lives. Through the knowledge of programs and the needs of these individuals, a better understanding of these persons will help younger generations be more comfortable in dealing with them and with the issues involving them.

My husband always viewed his disability as a conquerable challenge. The pain, the lack of total freedom, the inconvenience, and the constant interruption of daily life were treated largely as a nuisance. He continued to love life, his family, his career, the out-of-doors. His severe permanent disability never prevented his pursuit of life or dampened his tremendous sense of humor.

From the great number of disabled veterans, we have received the priceless gift of time for whatever reason their destiny was left to fulfill.

For my husband, Lee, his life DID make a profound difference to so many people who knew him.

Just seconds before the fateful claymore mine blasted his legs, Lee saw it and pushed a fellow soldier, Bill Bowden, out of harm's way. Bill called and thanked Lee years later. Sammy Jackson courageously scooped Lee up over his shoulders and carried him to safety. Enemy snipers opened fire on the wounded, shooting Lee twice in the back. His body was put with the dead until an alert medic saw his chest move. Fire hoses were used to get the thick, black rice paddy mud off of the maimed bodies. Exposure to Agent Orange and the other mysterious herbicides slowly took their toll. Terrible infections with high fevers were just another rung on the ladder to possible recovery.

Driving with hand controls for the rest of his life, Lee rarely took a handicapped parking space. He would admonish me, saying someone else needed it more. Embarrassingly and always without fail, the bullet in his heart would set off the security alarms at the airports. His dying, suddenly and unexpectedly, was typical, as he never wanted a fuss about himself. Proudly, his three children and I, along with other family members witnessed his name added to the Wall (18th panel West, 37th line) in November 1995. We strongly sense his spirit resting there, finding peace. All disabled veterans have their own stories; all have their own places in history.

To all post-Vietnam War generations, I urge you to look past the disability you can or cannot see and into the inner person. Visit the Vietnam Veterans Memorial—see it, touch it, and feel its power. There are many veterans, disabled or not, who will gladly attempt to fulfill your need to understand and theirs to teach; listen and learn—and help the healing to go on.

Mary B. Schaaf, R.N., B.S.N, C.S.N, S.N.P, M.Ed., is the widow of Lee R. Schaaf, who served with Bravo Company, 199th Light Infantry Brigade. They were married for 19 1/2 years and have three children: Christopher, Alme, and Ryan. Mary is a school nurse at Garwood Middle School in Fairview High School in Fairview, Pennsylvania. She worked diligently to have Lee's name added to the Vietnam Veterans Memorial after his sudden death on February 1990. His death was a direct result from the injuries sustained in the Vietnam War.

BY JACK SMITH

Nothing is so precious to a nation as its youth. And so, to squander the lives of the young in a war one is not prepared to win is crazy. Yet, that's exactly what happened in Vietnam.

It was mostly teenagers who were soldiers. And nearly 60,000 of them died and 300,000 were hurt, some horribly, in a war the U.S. fought in a way that it couldn't be won. What a waste. That is why so many Vietnam veterans still feel bitter.

Nothing is so drastic as war. If you're going to fight, fight all out. But in Vietnam, we were never committed to the war. And led by President Lyndon Johnson—one of our greatest domestic leaders, but in foreign affairs one of our most naïve—we escalated piecemeal. We were too timid to carry the fight to the enemy until the end, and tried to keep the war contained to South Vietnam.

The result was that the enemy, a small country waging total war (using all its resources), saw a super-power fighting a limited war, and concluded that if it could just sustain the 10-to-1 casualties for a while (after all, North Vietnam produced babies faster than we could kill its soldiers), then we would tire and leave and it would win. Of course, Ho Chi Minh was right. In 1968, we quit and began the longest and costliest retreat in American history. As Dean Rusk, the then-Secretary of State, later ruefully admitted: "They outlasted us." The fact is, democracies don't fight inconclusive wars for remote goals in distant places for very long.

Contrast this with how the Gulf War was fought: the Bush administration took just six months to put 500,000 troops in the Gulf. And Bush wasn't afraid to let his generals fight the war their way. What did they need to win? A shallow invasion of Iraq? Politically dangerous, but never mind, let them do it. And so the U.S. won decisively with almost no casualties.

Lyndon Johnson, on the other hand, harnessed his generals to a basically civilian policy—fighting the war piecemeal so nobody in the U.S. would notice. As for the enemy, he treated Ho Chi Minh like a member of the political opposition: show him the U.S. was tougher and he'd give up. But Ho saw the incrementalism that resulted as weakness and hung on. Tens of thousands of young Americans died needlessly.

I weep for my dead friends. I will never forget them. If you have to fight a war and spill blood, fight it to *win* or don't fight at all. That's the sad lesson of Vietnam.

Jack Smith is a TV correspondent for ABC News, based in Washington, D.C. He was a soldier in Vietnam, and was wounded in 1965 in the Ia Drang Valley when his unit was overrun and suffered more than 90% casualties in one of the bloodiest battles of the war.

BY BARBARA SONNEBORN

On February 29, 1968, early in the morning, near Que Sanh, Vietnam, Jeff Gurvitz, my childhood sweetheart and young husband, crawled out of a foxhole during a mortar attack to try to rescue his wounded radio operator. Both of them were killed, along with four other men. Multiple metal fragment wounds, they told me. That news shattered my life.

On January 1, 1988, I awoke, suddenly compelled to make a statement about Jeff's death in Vietnam. I realized that in all those years I had met only one other widow of the Vietnam War. I began to wonder: Where are these women? How have these terrible losses affected their lives? What do these women have to say about war? And most importantly, what can be learned from all these tragic deaths? So, I started to write a letter to Jeff, to begin to tell him the impact his death had on my life. That letter has evolved into "Regret To Inform"—a documentary film in which Vietnam War widows from *both sides* of the conflict becomes a lens, through which we can examine war and its devastating long term effects on individuals, society, and the environment.

In the process of working on this film, I have traveled across America and to Vietnam, to try to understand what happens when a country chooses to go to war. One of the American widows that I interviewed told me, "It's not just the war itself. It's the aftereffects of the war. It isn't just the war is here and then it's over. That isn't where it ends. It starts when it ends, when you're trying to rebuild yourself and your life."

After World War II, General Dwight D. Eisenhower stated, "Someday people are going to want peace so bad that governments are going to have to give it to them." The truth of this statement lies in the people; that is, each individual is responsible for war or peace.

The Vietnam War was the most unpopular of all wars. It was the most difficult war to explain. During the Vietnam War, the nation became dispirited, and those who served and those who lost loved ones were left with the question, "Did I fight in vain?" "Did my beloved die in vain?" Agonizing questions. Many hid the fact of their service or their loss. They suffered alone, in isolation. I have been told by many widows about the anonymous phone calls they received. "I'm glad your husband was killed; he was a baby murderer!" Or, "Anyone stupid enough to fight in this war deserved to die!" Instead of victory parades, we saw soldiers returning from Vietnam with curses and rotten tomatoes being thrown at them.

During the Vietnam War, a generation of young men and women answered the call of their nation with the patriotism and courage that have characterized the youth of this nation from its beginning. They were blamed, instead of embraced, and many still suffer the consequences of that betrayal.

There was an enormous discrepancy, as we look at the Vietnam War, between what those in control of our government said we were doing and what we actually were doing in Vietnam. As the protests increased, more and more people questioned why our young men were dying there. At that time, few people were even concerned with the losses Vietnam suffered, which is an important concept in "Regret to Inform."

We dehumanized the "other side," so we could kill them. In the case of the Vietnam War, we called the Vietnamese, a proud people with an ancient heritage, "gooks." We were told they didn't value life as much as we did, and so on.

I interviewed Vietnamese war widows throughout Vietnam, women who lost not only their husbands, but their whole families, their houses, water buffaloes, and land. They wept over their shattered lives—the same salty tears the American widows wept.

We closed our hearts and minds to the humanity of an entire people that were not threatening our shores. Closed hearts and minds are dangerous weapons.

What can we learn from all this loss today? I believe that the Vietnam War ended an era of blind faith in our government. Our biggest danger is the return of that blind faith with a new generation. We were lied to by our government. Those lies got us embroiled in that bitter and tragic war. And we are and will be lied to again and again, unless we demand the truth, unless we educate ourselves. If we do not understand our history, we are doomed to repeat our mistakes.

Since human beings crept out of their caves and bashed in the skulls of their neighbors with clubs, we have been solving problems in the same fashion with increasingly sophisticated weaponry.

As we move into the 21st century, it is time to see that we, the people, can and must demand new, non-violent solutions to conflict. We have seen, in the 20th century, that we have the potential to destroy the entire human race with war, quite easily, actually. It is up to you.

Barbara Sonneborn, widowed in 1968, is a filmmaker who continues to explore the often ignored plight of war widows through her art.

BY STEPHEN SOSSAMAN

For me, the main lesson for individual students to learn is what the nation, in general, learned from the Vietnam War: individual citizens must not surrender their own judgment in the assumption that government leaders know best. Sometimes, those leaders are ignorant, immoral, self-serving, stupid, blinded by ideology or pride, or just plain wrong in their judgments.

I'm not encouraging cynicism, just a healthy skepticism and a determination to educate oneself.

In the Vietnam War, as always, some leaders made honest mistakes. Others lied about decisions made for their own interest. In any event, many Vietnamese and Americans lost their lives, their wholeness, or their loved ones because our government and some military leaders made many mistakes. These mistakes, which were in themselves tragic, were based on erroneous judgments.

Many blunders were made because government and military leaders never bothered to learn about the Vietnamese history or culture. The arrogance of civilians, like Robert McNamara, and some military leaders cost other people their lives.

Other mistakes were made because some powerful people were less interested in the good of our nation than they were in their personal political fortunes or their political parties' success. Some historians and veterans believe that the war was prolonged by Richard Nixon and Henry Kissinger to enhance the 1972 re-election campaign. Some POWs were also believed to have been knowingly left behind. The Pentagon made some decisions that were not based on battlefield requirements, but on budgetary struggles and inter-service rivalry. Too many officers put their careers ahead of their mission and the lives of their men. People died as a result.

People learn best when they first realize that they do not know very much. Most of the veterans thought we knew what was happening when we entered Vietnam. But we were profoundly shocked and troubled to discover that the reality of the war was not as it had been told to us. Some of the veterans have never recovered from this confusion and disorientation.

American soldiers and civilians were repeatedly lied to by our government. We were deluded about the nature of the war and the secret of American involvement in the war's early years. The few who tried to educate us were ridiculed and named unpatriotic.

Schools, too often, perpetuate ignorance and blind trust, by reinforcing positive myths about America, instead of trusting students with the truth. The book titled Lies My Teacher Told Me demonstrates this mis-education—read the chapter on how the Vietnam War is not taught.

Never again, should an American offer to kill, risk death, or support a war, as voters, unless there is good reason to believe that the war is both unavoidable and just. This decision requires self-education about history, current events, and different cultures.

Some Vietnam veterans are proud of serving in what they consider a noble cause. Others consider the war immoral. Nearly all veterans agree that we were not treated honestly or wisely by our government.

Stephen Sossaman was in the 9th Infantry Division artillery in Vietnam during 1968. A Professor of English at Westfield State College in Massachusetts, he is also a speaker and trainer for the Veterans Education Project.

BY JOHN O. WOODS, JR.

When I said goodbye to my parents, brothers, and sister in mid-August 1967, I was not sure that I would ever return. But I believed that this was an opportunity to both serve my country and help the people in a small country to have the same freedom of choice in determining the type of government they wanted. I shared President Johnson's "guns and butter" philosophy that we could both fight a war and continue our prosperity and way of life at home. In fact, I remember responding to my aunt's letter in which she regretted planning a party while I could be killed. I had grown up believing that each of us has an obligation to protect our great country and all of our freedoms. I wrote to her saying that she should not regret having a party; I was only trying to make sure that she would never lose the freedom to have that party, as well as give the Vietnamese that same chance.

After only six weeks in-country, I woke up in a hospital bed in Long Bihn. I was very disappointed when my aviation company commander congratulated me on a job well done and informed me that I had just won a free, all-expense-paid trip back home. I had not even begun to succeed at my personal mission. Unlike many of my comrades, I came "home" in December to Andrews AFB, outside of Washington, on a medivac C-141. I was welcomed by a USAF Colonel who said I had my own private ambulance to Walter Reed Army Hospital. Upon my request, the Army medic driving the ambulance took me to Walter Reed by way of the Capitol, down Pennsylvania Avenue, and past the White House. Tears of joy flowed during the entire trip at the sight of these beautiful monuments and the U.S. flags flying in the starlit night.

During the course of the next three years of my recovery, I was often angered by the demonstrations against the war by the young people, which was egged on by many elected members of the Congress debating the justification of Vietnam. This was going on, to my disbelief, while patients without arms, legs, or sometimes eyes arrived weekly at Walter Reed, and while we would read or watch the body count in the press and on television. Unfortunately, this debate should have occurred many years earlier, before a single U.S. soldier left the country for Vietnam.

In 1991, our success in Kuwait during Desert Storm confirmed many thoughts gained or observed over my life—not only in Vietnam, but between 1970 and 1991:

> We can never commit the troops unless we commit the American people; there must be a shared sacrifice to sense the importance of our purpose.
>
> Politicians must never be allowed to conduct a war. They are neither qualified nor have the proper perspective to make the kind of decisions that war requires. We observed the success when professional soldiers, like General Schwarzkopf and his other officers, were shown the confidence of President Bush and the American people. These professional soldiers were given the opportunity to demonstrate their training and expertise, just like a trial lawyer or surgeon.
>
> Contrary to the glorification and excitement of war that movies and books tend to portray, we must understand that war is not a game conducted under rules or with fair play—young people are killed, disabled, wounded physically and mentally, and often tortured. Because we have not seen a modern war on our own soil, we must encourage all Americans to visit the rest of the world, preferably in person, or via the media. Americans will not only develop a sense of how war destroys the physical features of these war-torn countries, but develop a real appreciation for how much we have in the United States in comparison.

Through teaching the history of those who have sacrificed their lives and fortunes in America, we must develop an accountability and sense of patriotism among future generations. Future generations must be willing to make the individual sacrifice in order to protect our freedoms. We cannot let it be the "other guy," nor can we always have absolute assurance that our leaders' decisions are correct. Our great country is built on the trust in God and each other.

John O. Woods, Jr., U.S. Army Captain, served in Vietnam from 9/67 through 10/67 as a UH-1 "Huey" pilot until he was shot down. He recovered from his injuries and retired for disability in 1970. He is now the Vice President of FDE, Ltd., Consulting Engineers, a structural engineering firm in Alexandria, Virginia.

BY GEORGE WORTHINGTON

The most important thing to learn from the Vietnam War is that our elected officials must be held accountable for their decisions, especially when American service lives are at stake.

The Vietnam War was the most divisive event in the United States this century—just as the Civil War was in the last. The principles at issue in each were (and remain) momentous to the body politic of the nation. In the Civil War, the central issue was slavery and the rights of states to secede from the Union. The excuse in Vietnam was communist aggression. The issue, however, was blurred in the eyes of our national leadership, which failed to understand the nature of the conflict, its underlying causes, or the culture. United States policy was driven by the simplistic "domino theory," which held if one country fell to communism, the whole region would succumb. From Presidents Eisenhower, Kennedy, and Johnson, to Nixon, the strategy was flawed.

Apart from trying to answer the questions "Why?" and "How?", what has evolved over the twenty years since the end of the Vietnam War and the American pullout is greater understanding of accountability of our elected representatives and the military commanders in charge of the combat effort. Not one elected official, however, was punished for his decisions in Vietnam—unless one considers Lyndon Johnson's not running for a second term as "punishment." Only one senior military decision-maker was held accountable, Air Force General John Lavelle, for his secret bombing of the North.

Dissension over foreign wars has existed throughout America's past. Citizens have protested all of the country's armed engagements, from the Revolutionary War forward. Before World War II, many people did not want to fight against Germany, and more recently, a near majority questioned our involvement in the Persian Gulf War. Today, many of us are opposed to U.S. presence in Bosnia. But America had never "lost" a shooting war until Vietnam. Regardless of the case made by a few revisionists that we did not lose on the battlefield, *per se*, but in the halls of Washington and Saigon, American political objectives were not met. American policy was defeated, and it has taken us twenty years to come to grips with the question of how could we have been so misled in our foreign policy and defense strategy.

Military historians are only lately coming to grips with the issue of accountability for United States decisions in Vietnam. Retired Army Colonel David Hackworth in his About Face (1989) and Robert Asprey's War In The Shadows (1994) are two works that investigate in depth the rationale surrounding America's entry into Vietnam—first, to shore up the ill-fated French effort and, later, to repeat the same errors, tactically and strategically, after the French got out.

Apart from the support role the United States played in what is now known as the First Indochina War (December 19, 1946–May 8, 1954)—funding upwards of 80% of the French costs—the United States unilateral involvement in Vietnam began modestly in 1955. American aid and advice, however, could not prevent the country's downward political slide into dictatorship and repression. Had the Johnson Administration only read Bernard Fall's Street Without Joy and The Two Vietnams: A Political and Military Analysis in 1963, when the two works were published, they might have proceeded with greater knowledge of the region's political problems and, hence, greater prudence. Who knows, maybe the Wall would not have been necessary.

Unfortunately, all U.S. "Vietnam Administrations" were consumed by communist paranoia. Clearly vision was occluded: mistakes were made over and over with no clear strategy for the political reforms obviously needed since 1955 and, worse—from the standpoint of lives lost on both sides, many of which were innocent civilians—by tactically fighting the wrong kind of war, i.e., military commanders tried to force European firepower tactics onto a guerrilla war scenario. The American strategy of attrition evidenced by the compilation of "body counts" was totally wrong and may have extended the conflict, which always had sought a political solution and could never be won on a battlefield without resorting to extraordinary measures, e.g., nuclear. We proved this beyond anyone's question, as in the end U.S. withdrawal was negotiated—why in 1973, and not in 1963, is food for further study by scholars and historians.

Accordingly, the abiding issue to be taken away from the Vietnam War by all Americans is that our elected officials, and the military and naval commanders they appoint, must be held accountable for their decisions. VIETNAM, NEVER AGAIN!

Rear Admiral George R. Worthington, U.S. Navy (Retired), initially saw service in Vietnam in 1965 on the Navy staff responsible for establishing the Market Time patrol barriers of South Vietnam. Later, in 1966 and 1967, as a "frogman" with the Navy's famed Underwater Demolition Teams, he participated in coastal reconnaissance missions. He served in 1971 on the Naval Special Warfare Group (Vietnam), responsible for U.S. Navy SEAL Team operations. He saw a final tour in Southeast Asia as the U.S. Naval Attaché to Cambodia, in Phnom Penh, and witnessed that country's fall in April 1975. He works today as a consultant and has visited Vietnam on two occasions and has established business contacts in Hanoi and Ho Chi Minh City.

WHY VIETNAM STILL MATTERS

The Wall

BY ANONYMOUS

At the Wall, a computer database is available to help Vietnam veterans, family, and friends find the name of someone killed or missing in the war. Volunteers can perform searches by name, rank, hometown, service branch, casualty date, birth date, even a combination of these categories. But in the early days of the Memorial, all we had was the Wall and the paperback directory to perform a search. It was not unusual to spend extended periods of time attempting to assist a vet who could not remember his buddy's real name. In many cases, they knew each other only by nicknames.

During the spring of 1995, the day before Memorial Day, a vet who was looking for his buddy, whom he had been told had been killed, arrived at the Memorial. He remembered that his last name began with an "I," a letter in the alphabet that did not have many entries in the directory. We sat on a bench, just down from the information kiosk, and looked through all of the "I's" in an effort to find the name for which he was looking. Nothing sounded familiar to him. He left in a mood that reflected his frustration at the unsuccessful search. As one can well imagine, sitting with someone attempting to find their buddy was not an uncommon experience for a volunteer working at the Vietnam Veterans Memorial. There was nothing unusual about this effort. It had become routine.

A few hours and many name searches later, another vet came up to try and find his buddy who had been killed after he left Vietnam. As I recall, the last name began with an "R." We began to look for the name, but he wasn't really sure what his name was, all he knew for sure was his nickname. Patience was not with him that day and he chose to leave before we had completed going through the letter of the last name.

Time flies when volunteering at the Wall, especially during the holidays. It is both exciting and tiring. I was just about ready to leave as I had been there for over ten hours.

As I was walking up from the Wall, I saw the vet I had worked with earlier that day. He asked if I remembered him. I remembered the face and sitting on the bench with him looking through the letter "I." As we were chatting, another vet came up to say something to me. It was the one who was looking for a name beginning with "R." He excused himself to the vet I was speaking with, as he wanted to say goodbye to me. They looked at each other and called each other by nickname. One was the vet we were looking for under the letter "I", and the other was the vet we were looking for under the letter "R." They had found each other, but not on the Wall as they had expected. They found each other alive in the flesh.

I walked away as they renewed their friendship knowing that had I not been there to assist in their searches, the timing might not have been right for them to meet that day. On the way back to the kiosk, feeling like all of the blood had been drained from my body, I passed our volunteer coordinator. She asked me what happened, saying that I looked like I had seen a ghost. I felt like I had seen two. It was two weeks before I returned to volunteer.

BY DAN ARANT

Late in the afternoon on September 5, 1993, I was standing near the vertex of the Wall, preparing myself to head home and waiting for a break in the flow of visitors. My other VVM Volunteer colleagues were helping visitors on the East Wall, in the direction of the Washington Monument. A young couple, silhouetted by the setting sun, approached from the west, in the direction of the Lincoln Memorial. I decided to wait and see whether they had any questions for me.

They walked past me and stopped near the edge of the grass in front of the second panel on the East Wall.

They faced the panel, she in front, he in back, with his arms wrapped around her. From a respectful distance, I watched as tears began to flow freely down the woman's cheeks. They stood perfectly still for what seemed like fifteen minutes. My first thought was what a poignant photograph this would make, but I was soon mesmerized by the unfolding scene.

The spell was broken when the young woman walked up to the Wall and laid a bouquet of flowers at the base of panel 2E. She stepped back and the two resumed their previous pose – this time, however, her head was tucked securely into his shoulder. Ten minutes passed. It was like a scene from a frieze on a Grecian urn, the stillness broken only by the tears flowing down their cheeks. A new visitor claimed my attention to find the name of a loved one in my directory. After finding the name, I looked up and saw the couple walking east into the shadows made by the fading sun.

I walked up to the bouquet. A small handwritten note was attached loosely to one of the flower stems. It read:

To: Lee Roy James
Killed September 5, 1965
Dear Dad,

Yesterday, your baby girl married a wonderful, wonderful man. Although I did not see you there, I felt your

presence in my heart and in the hearts of your family and friends. I am leaving you the flowers I carried down the aisle when Tom escorted me. It should have been you. I love you.
Always, Tina Leigh

I secured the note to the bouquet; it was too precious to risk having it blown away. I stayed a while longer; it was almost sunset, but the tears in the eyes of the visitors who read the note were clearly visible.

I keep a copy of this note in my name listing-book. It reflects my idea of what the Wall is all about.

Postscript: Lee Roy James was a Gunnery Sergeant in the Marine Corps. His "baby girl" visited the Memorial twenty-eight years to the day after his death and had been married the day before.

Daniel R. Arant served in Vietnam as a Navy lieutenant with the U.S. Vietnam Naval Advisory Group in 1968, and volunteers at the Vietnam Veterans Memorial. He returned to Vietnam in 1995 with Global Volunteers, a St. Paul, MN-based international community service organization, and helped to construct a security wall for a village preschool and to teach English at a village night school in the Mekong Delta. He looks forward to returning to Vietnam again.

BY TOM BAXTER

It was early on a quiet spring Sunday morning with few visitors making their way through the Memorial, when a young lady asked for the location of a name and requested a rubbing. The location was on one of the smaller panels of the East Wall which necessitated my kneeling to do the rubbing. As I proceeded with the rubbing, I inquired as to the relationship between them—if it was a family member, friend or neighbor. She knelt down beside me, held one edge of the paper and said, in a soft southern accent, "We went to school together. He took me to our senior prom and that night he gave me my first kiss. Soon after graduation, he went into the service, then to Vietnam and I never saw him again."

When we arose, she thanked me and gave me a hug. There were tears in her eyes but a delicate smile on her lips. She turned and walked slowly back down through the Memorial and out the West exit. It was the most poignant few moments I've experienced during my time at the Wall.

Tom Baxter, a World War II and Korean Navy veteran, has been a volunteer at the Vietnam Veterans Memorial for 13 years and was named 1994 Volunteer of the Year.

BY JOHN BENDER

I've worked as a volunteer guide at the Vietnam Veterans Memorial since it was dedicated. I've heard stories of heroism and cowardice, of pride in what was done and of regret for things not done. But the story which continues to haunt me started in the most innocuous way.

I spotted a young woman who seemed to be searching the Wall for a name. She was in her mid-twenties, an Asian-American, and a truly beautiful woman. I asked if I could help her.

She was looking for her father's name and couldn't find it in the *Directory of Names*. The name began with an "Mc" and I knew there were several places where the name might appear. I checked them with no success. I asked if she knew the date of casualty and we located the names from that day on the Wall. But his name was not there. I checked my list of names added—it was not there.

I began to suspect that the father's death did not meet the criteria. For example, he might have died while on R and R in Australia. I questioned the young woman.

No, there had been no official notification. Her mother was Vietnamese, her father was a helicopter crew member, and they were not legally married. Just before she was born, her father's buddies had told her mother that her father had been killed in a helicopter crash.

What should I tell this young woman? Should I tell her there is no way that a soldier killed in a helicopter crash in Vietnam would not be listed in the *Directory*? Or should I leave her, and her mother, with the story they had been told and which they believed—that the father had not deserted them but had died heroically?

I'm still troubled by this matter. Did I do the right thing? What, in actuality, did I do? I gave her some suggestions as to how she might find her father. I hope that she found him and that they came to know and love each other. But who knows?

John Bender has been a volunteer since 1982 when the Memorial was dedicated. He served during World War II as a Coast Guard reserve officer, and his son, wounded and decorated in Vietnam, is a colonel with the Marine Reserves.

BY FRANK BOSCH

In the over thirteen years that I have been a volunteer at the Memorial, there have been hundreds of sad and interesting moments. Of the thousands of people with whom I have met and chatted, I can recall many. Some were relatives of those lost in the war, some were celebrities, and some from various levels of the government. I've met visitors from foreign countries, and a myriad of others, including military people (active, retired or veterans), scholars, business people, and school children. Everyone seems to make their way to the Memorial.

My normal day at the Memorial is Wednesday. It is not as busy as on the weekends or holidays which affords me more time to spend with the visitors and to provide more personalized attention than when there are crowds all seeking my help.

One day, several years ago, a young man came to me and asked if I could help him locate a friend of his, a routine thing. I proceeded, as usual, to ask for the person's name and immediately found the name of the soldier on the Memorial Wall.

In looking for the panel and line number, I noticed that the soldier was from New Orleans, Louisiana. Since I was born in New Orleans, I asked the visitor if he was from there as well, to which he replied, "Yes." I then asked him, "Where in New Orleans?" "Well, not exactly in New Orleans, but across the river in Gretna."

Once again, I asked the "Where?" question. "Appletree Lane." "Where on Appletree Lane?" By then, he was looking a little quizzical but he said, "300 Appletree Lane." I smiled and said that my eldest sister lived at 339 Appletree Lane. Both surprised, we started to compare data and yes, he knew my sister and her husband by sight and was familiar with their home. Then, he started asking the questions.

The young man asked my name and I gave it to him and told him that there were no living Bosches in New Orleans but I had a number of relatives there. In fact, the boulevard leading to the Super Dome was named after my mother's first cousin, Earhart Boulevard. It was here that I thought I was going to lose him because he came back with, "*My* mother's maiden name was Earhart also!" We both were amazed because neither one of us had had any inkling that we could possibly be related. We finally ascertained that we were many, many cousins removed and we have a tentative date to get together the next time I visit New Orleans.

While I did not know the soldier on the Wall, this is just one of many examples of how the Wall can bring people together. I used to call people, "Cousin" as a means of a friendly greeting, but I don't do that anymore because the next one might truly be my cousin!

Frank Bosch, Lt. Col. USAF (retired) is a veteran of 34 years in the United States Army Air Corps and the United States Air Force. He has been volunteering at the Memorial since its dedication. He has had the good fortune to meet many people whom he had served with over the years and has even discovered some on the Memorial he had not known had been killed or declared missing.

BY KATHY FERGUSON

One balmy February Sunday, I was at the Wall as a volunteer with the National Park Service. It was a fairly busy day and as I finished doing a rubbing for a visitor, a gentleman approached me. He asked if I would do a rubbing for him. He was a well-dressed Hispanic man, probably in his late '50s, and quite shy. I followed him to the panel where he showed me the name. As I was doing the rubbing he asked if I would mind doing six of them—they were for a very poor family in California who hadn't been able to visit the Wall.

While I worked, he told me the young man was one of twins, that they had both gone to Vietnam and the other one had returned unharmed. When I finished and handed him the rubbings and some brochures, he asked if I would please do one more thing for him. He wanted me to take two photographs of his fingers placed over the name. He said the young man's mother had kissed his fingers and he wanted to record that he had placed that kiss on his name. All I could do was nod that I would.

I don't know what relation this man is to the mother. He could be a family member, friend, neighbor or employer; but that isn't important. What's important is that somewhere in California there is a Lopez family that has found some comfort and closure to their grief through this man's visit to the Wall.

Kathy Ferguson has been working as a volunteer at the Vietnam Veterans Memorial since 1989 because she wanted to give something back to those who had served their country during this difficult time. She has been helping VVMF provide name rubbings for those people who aren't able to make the trip to the Wall themselves.

BY GERTRUDE GERBER

He was stooping, gazing at the Wall. It was apparent he was very tall. I watched him off and on as he stood for a very long time, perhaps an hour or more. I wondered—had he served in Vietnam, lost a brother, a classmate? Should I intrude on his remembrances? Yet, I was concerned. He had been stooping, seemingly motionless, for such a very long time.

Finally, with all the nerve I could muster, I walked toward him and asked if I could do a rubbing for him. Ever so quietly, he said, "No, thank you, but would it be all right if I read a poem to *my men*?"

"Of course," I answered. "Would you like your privacy or may I listen?"

"You may listen," he answered. He rose, took a sheet of paper from his pocket, unfolded it, looked at the Wall, then began to read. It was a long poem, and he delivered it eloquently.

As he folded the sheet of paper that had held a tribute to "his men," he once again gazed at the mirror-like surface of the Wall. He seemed contented. Then he turned toward me, kissed me on the cheek, and quietly walked away.

I knew once again, why I had come to the Wall as a volunteer. "His men," like their buddies, gave their lives. I could give my time.

Gertrude Gerber saw an advertisement for volunteers in The Washington Post and knowing what a "bum rap" the Vietnam veterans had gotten, felt it was something she could do for them. Which is exactly what she has been doing Tuesdays ever since the spring of 1983.

BY ALAN GROPMAN

On Veterans Day 1992, I received an insight regarding the Vietnam War that has remained with me since, and probably will stay with me forever—I learned that the war had not ended for many people.

I became involved in commemorating the 10th Anniversary of the Memorial Wall by conducting a symposium on the Vietnam War. I was teaching strategy at the Industrial College of the Armed Forces, one of the two war colleges at the National Defense University. I served two flying tours in Vietnam and over the years had published a book, several anthology chapters, and several shorter writings on the Vietnam War. When I taught at the War College, I had directed core courses for two years on the war.

These classes were unique because no academics spoke to the students (who were senior military and civilian officials), only practitioners—Walt Whitman Rostow, Elmo Zumwalt, William Colby, Robert Komer, Leslie Gelb, and other decision-makers spoke.

For the Wall's commemoration symposium, I used those courses as a model in the conduct of our symposium: The Vietnam War and the post Vietnam War Military. We heard from chiefs or senior officers during or after the Vietnam War who were also combat veterans of that conflict. Edward Meyer, Elmo Zumwalt, Michael Dugan, and Philip Shutler could all speak about how the war affected their forces.

Because of my efforts in arranging this symposium, Jan Scruggs asked me to read names at the Wall in November 1992. Like all of those so privileged, I arrived before the appointed time to rehearse my reading because I was informed that parents and spouses and children of those who are memorialized might be present, and no one wanted to mispronounce a name. I practiced the names and took my place at the foot of the platform on which the readers stood. There were five readers in front of me. None of them were veterans of the conflict because all were obviously too young.

I was not clearly a veteran either—I was dressed in my best suit and overcoat (it was about 8:00 PM and cold and damp).

Each of the readers read their designated list and departed the stage without incident. When I finished reading my list of names, however, I identified the men in my outfit—the 463 Tactical Airlift Wing—who had been killed during my second Vietnam tour, February 1968 to May 1969, and whose names were on the Wall. I recited Jim McKinistry, L.R. Stow, Bernie Bucher, John McElroy and a dozen others and turned to leave the stage, but could not because from out of the darkness appeared twenty men dressed in fatigues who surrounded me, embraced me, and said: "Welcome back." The Vietnam War had not ended for them; and for that moment, it had not ended for me either.

Dr. Alan Gropman is a retired Air Force colonel, currently teaching at the Industrial College of the Armed Forces. He served 27 years in the Air Force, including two Vietnam tours, and accumulated 671 combat missions.

BY LIBBY HATCH

There was a steady flow of visitors to the Wall that day. Some were walking slowly but never pausing, some stopping at a panel and rubbing their fingers on a name and then moving away. One figure caught my eye as he stood as far from the Wall as he could, the backs of his legs rubbing the chain which kept pedestrian traffic from spilling off the sidewalk. This young man stood holding the item he would later proffer to the father he barely remembered, mute and motionless, staring at his dad's name for ten minutes, at least. Only after the young man put down the collage of family photos, news articles, a letter written in crayon, all protected by plastic, and stood back away from the panel, did I see the tears that had started to roll down his face.

I wandered off but after what must have been five more minutes, he saw me as I was glancing at him out of the corner of my eye, and I smiled tentatively. I wanted to take a photograph of him and the item he had obviously spent a lot of time putting together in offering, but I did not want to disturb his contemplation. He indicated that he would not mind being photographed, and yet when I asked if he would like me to send him a copy, he said no. He was still living at home and his mother wouldn't want to see it. He explained that while she visits her husband's grave site back home, she could not bring herself to visit the Wall—it was still just too raw for her. As for him, though, whenever he went to the cemetery, he felt that his father was with a bunch of dead people. It was only at the Wall that his dad was with friends.

Libby Hatch has worked for the Vietnam Veterans Memorial Fund since 1991, as project director for the 10th Anniversary Commemoration of the Dedication of the Vietnam Veterans Memorial, and continues as VVMF administrator.

BY BOBBIE KEITH

Morning dew sprinkled a rainbow of colors across the Wall as the sun's first ray glistened upon the black granite panels. Crisp, cool air whispered through trees. Squirrels pranced upon a blanket of colored leaves.

On such a Fall morning, I noticed a lean, blue-jeaned figure hunched on a park bench. I met Matt. He had kept vigil throughout the night—lighting candle after candle in memory of his Navy buddy. When his last candle finally lost its flame, he stood, saluted and quietly retreated.

Later that morning, as I sat in the warmth of the information kiosk, I searched for what Matt had dropped in my carry-all bag—only to find a crumpled up piece of paper. It read:

In the shadow of your footsteps
I walk with you tonight
with memories kindled bright
by the flame of candle light

Dennis (a Park Ranger who had also served in Vietnam) and I simultaneously took a deep breath and sighed to keep any tears from forming as we discussed how what we had just read may explain Matt's pilgrimage to the Wall; that perhaps he wanted us to understand his thoughts through the poem he had written.

Fall after Fall, Matt would return to continue the candle-light vigil he began in 1983. That early Fall morning is but one of a mosaic of heartwarming images developed through time as a volunteer at the Wall.

Today, I still have that crumpled up piece of paper. Framed, it captures many of the emotions shared at the Wall.

Bobbie Keith was employed by the U.S. Agency for International Development (USAID) and was posted in Vietnam from 1967-1969. Many veterans will remember her as

"Bobbie the Weathergirl," who did the nightly weather broadcasts for "Vietnam and Back Home in the Land of the Big PX." She continued her adventures working for the Department of State in Germany, Jordan, France, Turkey, Colombia, Morocco, and Canada among others. In her four years posted in Washington, DC, she worked as a NPS Volunteer at the Wall.

BY SUZANNE SIGONA

People often ask why I do this work. The most brief explanation for me is that I graduated from high school in 1968. All decisions we made then were related to Vietnam, the draft, and lives put on hold. I was married in 1969. My husband got drafted and although he did not go to Vietnam, we did not have a marriage when he returned from overseas. When people say to me, "I didn't lose anyone in Vietnam," I want to reply, "Then you aren't paying attention."

I've been at the Wall for eight years. Although I left Washington last year, I still remain involved with vets, their families, and the big puzzle that still has many pieces missing.

My introduction to the family of KC, one name on the Wall, came about seven years ago when a Vietnam buddy of his visited the Wall for the first time. We struck up a conversation, I helped him find KC's name, and exchanged addresses. Later, he wrote to me asking what I thought about his contacting KC's family. My counsel to him was to prepare for the range of reactions he might receive, and I forwarded the phone book page from KC's home town of record. He contacted me again several months later to tell me he had contacted the family. The words I'll always remember were, "I cried for the first time since Vietnam."

I was heading to the city where KC's family lives and I decided to look them up. Those who don't know the Wall might ask, "Why would they want to see you?" Those who do know this place realize that when you help to join a family with the last person to see their son alive, it is a remarkable experience. Since I had played a part in this, KC's mother and family opened their lives to me. We became friends and I learned a lot about KC and those he had left behind.

When I met KC's mother, she told me what little she knew about the baby her son had fathered. He and the child's mother had not had time to marry, and the mother had put the child up for adoption. KC's mom explained that she never wanted to disrupt anyone's life but after losing her son, finding her granddaughter became more important. She had made several attempts over the years but it was not a time when organizations cooperated, and adoption files had been closed.

We worked to find her grandchild for literally years. We did the dance that is common to this process. Make progress and become frightened. Move forward again and as you celebrate a minor step forward, you hit a major roadblock.

Finally, I made a commitment to head to the state capital with Grandmother and Grandfather and go through whatever files were available. We had a few clues and a great deal of determination. We finally ended up at the home where the mother of her grandchild lived while she waited for the birth of "Christine," the name I arbitrarily gave her since we had no idea of either her first or last name. On that day, we did not get all the answers but we knew we were on the road to success.

Although this account does not begin to reveal all the layers of emotions that accompanied this pilgrimage, a peak was reached one evening when I got a call from "Grandma" telling me to sit down. She had just gotten off the phone with her granddaughter.

We thought we were in the early stages of our journey four or five years ago. In fact, we were just beginning the day we found her. Since that time, this "child" has had the opportunity that few sons and daughters ever have. She was able to visit the Vietnam Veterans Memorial with her grandmother and her father's buddies from Vietnam.

I've always believed that the work at the Wall is the most important thing I do in this life. Finding "Christine" has been the greatest part of that work. And do you want to know a funny thing? Her real name turned out to be Chris.

Suzanne Sigona has been working as a volunteer at the Wall for eight years.

BY RON STUFFLEBEAN

The Healing Place

Went to the Wall, this healing place
to renew friendships of old.
Went to see again the faces
that went with each name.
Went to speak their name and tell them
We have not forgotten.
But I will not cry.
As the firing squad, our places we took,
while memories from the past raced to present.
Raising our rifles, three volley of seven we fired
as the Colors waved in the breeze.
My throat tightened in awe of this healing place.
But I will not cry.
Taps sounded and my eyes gazed up and down
the length of the Wall.
A tear came to my eye—Had they seen,
those at this healing place?
But I will not cry.
Had I cheated them their due?
Later, moving up and down the length of
the Wall, lingering
Where a name and memory stirred emotions deep
I came upon a sister veteran. We talked -
we shared this healing place.
At long last I could not deny.
For at the Wall, I cried -- this healing place.

Ron Stufflebean volunteered and served one tour in Vietnam, 1968-69, with the 2nd Battalion, 17th Field Artillery, in II Corp, Central Highlands. His wife, Paula, served in the United States Air Force on bases from 1968–70. Ron and Paula volunteer at the Vietnam Veterans Memorial for the week before Veterans Day.

BY ALAN WALLACE

There have been many interesting and moving experiences for me working with the National Park Service as a volunteer at the Vietnam Veterans Memorial. Once, I was approached by a Marine veteran, in his mid-50s, who asked me to help him find the name of a friend. After finding the name, he also asked if I could look up six or seven others, adding that they had all been killed the same day. This told me that they were likely to all be listed on the same panel together. He was obviously grateful for my help in finding the names of his friends, from so many years past.

He thanked me, and asked if I had ever heard of Carlos Hathcock, USMC? (Hathcock had been a Marine sniper in Vietnam and wrote a book about it.) The Marine showed me a yellow business card with Hathcock's name, and the former sniper had signed his name on the back of it. He wanted to give me the card for helping him. I told him he should really keep it for himself. But he insisted that I have it, and so I accepted. He thanked me again and left. At about this time, my son, Keith, had been out of USMC Boot Camp for about four months. I gave the card to him, after I had it sealed in plastic. I am sure he will keep it along with his other USMC memorabilia, a precious token passed from Marine to Marine.

One of the more humorous incidents at the Wall occurs because of the reflective nature of the black granite. The Wall was designed to become part of its surroundings, reflecting the land, the sky, the monuments and indeed the people who are there to visit. Many times, when the weather is cold and sunny and the visitors are few, crows will walk around in the grassy area in front of the panels, flapping their wings and cawing loudly at their reflections. They fly away when visitors approach, only to return in a futile attempt to frighten their alter egos buried deep within the reflective stone. Everyone sees something different when they look into the Wall.

Alan Wallace, HM2 USN, has volunteered at the Vietnam Veterans Memorial since September 1993. He was on active duty with the Navy for four and a half years and served as an operating room technician in a combat hospital south of Da Nang from December 1967 to 1968. "The most intense time of my life. Not a day goes by that I don't think of my experiences there. I have often felt that I was never more valuable than when I was in Vietnam."

PRESIDENT JIMMY CARTER
Signing S.J. Res. 119 Into Law, at the Rose Garden, White House, Washington, D.C. July 1, 1980

Since I've been living in the White House and working in the Oval Office, I've known of very few unanimous resolutions or actions by the United States Senate. But it's especially fitting that this resolution and the effort to provide a suitable memorial for those who fought and died for our Nation during the Vietnam War, should have such broad and bipartisan support.

My wife, Rosalynn, for instance, has joined as one of the co-chairpersons, with many others, on the sponsoring committee of the Vietnam [Veterans] Memorial Fund.

I particularly want to acknowledge the dedication of Jan Scruggs, who began this effort formally, after years of preliminary work, in April of 1979, and the leadership of Senator Mathias, Senator Warner, Congressmen Bonior and Daschle and Chairman Bumpers and Chairman Nedzi and Congressman Hammerschmidt and many others who led the legislation successfully through the Congress.

I also want to congratulate and thank Secretary Cecil Andrus, who couldn't be here today, but whose agency supported and whose department will be responsible for the management and the maintenance of this monument; and for the Veterans Administrator, Max Cleland, who will speak to us in a few minutes, whose service to his country has continued since that war through today, and who joyfully celebrates his own "alive day" each year, because he knows better than most of us what it means to sacrifice and to serve and to suffer and to survive.

A long and a painful process has brought us to this moment today. Our Nation, as you all know, was divided by this war. For too long we tried to put that division behind us by forgetting the Vietnam War and, in the process, we ignored those who bravely answered their Nation's call, adding to their pain the additional burden of our Nation's own inner conflict.

Over the last 3 1/2 years, I have encouraged and I have been heartened to witness an enormous change in the attitude of Americans toward those who served in Vietnam. A Nation healing and reconciliation is a good sight to behold from the viewpoint of the Presidency, and we are ready at least to acknowledge more deeply and also more publicly the debt which we can never fully pay to those who served.

The word "honor" has been used so often and sometimes so carelessly—especially in public ceremonies—that there's a danger that it might lose its meaning. More importantly, we might forget what its true meaning is and, with it, the concept of duty and a standard of behavior and sense of humility that's precious and also irreplaceable. And when I say today that I am honored to be able to sign this resolution into law, I use that word with great care.

This is an important step toward the establishment of a permanent memorial for the young men and women who died in the service of our country in Vietnam; for those who, despite all our efforts, are still missing in Southeast Asia; and for all those who served and returned. We are honored to have a small part in offering this overdue recognition. They honored us and their country with their service, and no delay in recognizing them can lessen the value of their personal sacrifice.

Perhaps even more than those who served, our Nation needs this memorial as a reminder of what happened in the past, what was lost, and our need to learn from our experience. We need it also as a physical place where we can pay tribute to those young lives, what they meant, to kind of place apart, to recall the meaning of the word "honor," so that the word can retain all its simple and austere grandeur.

In honoring those who answered the call of duty, we do not honor war. But we honor the peace they sought, the freedoms that they fought to preserve, and the hope that they held out to a world that's still struggling to learn how to settle differences among people and among nations without resorting to violence.

All of us must be willing to sacrifice to protect freedom and to protect justice, but we are not called upon to sacrifice equally. In every war, there are some who are called on to make the ultimate sacrifice of their own lives. Some come home with bodies that must bear daily pain for the rest of their lives. A tragically large number were still missing when the war in Vietnam was over, and we'll continue to exert the fullest possible effort to account for all those who are still missing.

It's a pointless act of inhumanity and cruelty to prolong the vigil of those who love, waiting for those for so many years, and it's a vigil that's shared not just among the families directly, but shared by all Americans.

At the time of our White House reception in honor of Vietnam veterans last year, Phil Caputo, the author of A Rumor of War, permitted me to read from his book. I was greatly moved by this passage, as were the others at the time, and I feel it even more appropriate to read here today the same words that Caputo wrote in 1976, I believe, about the death of one of his close friends named Walter Levy, who was killed in Vietnam trying to save a fellow soldier and I quote:

> *"So much was lost with you, so much talent and intelligence and decency. You were the first from our class of 1964 to die. There were others, but you were the first and more: You embodied the best that was in us. You were a part of us, and a part of us died with you, the small part that was still young, that had not yet grown cynical, grown bitter and old with death. Your courage was an example to us, and whatever the rights or wrongs of the war, nothing can diminish the rightness of what you tried to do. Yours was the greater love. You died for the man you tried to save, and you died pro patria. It*

was not altogether sweet and fitting, your death, but I am sure you died believing it was pro patria. You were faithful."

To die for one's country is a sacrifice that should never be forgotten.

Caputo goes on to say that our country has not matched the faithfulness of that war hero, because our country tried to forget the war; that 11 years after his friend's death, Caputo wrote, there were no monuments, no statues, no plaques, no memorials, because such symbols would make it harder to forget.

I didn't read that part aloud last year. Now, we'll build a memorial to the Walter Levys who died on the other side of the world, sacrificing themselves for others, sacrificing themselves for us and for our children's children. With this memorial, we will say with Caputo: "We loved you for what you were and what you stood for." We will prove with this monument that we care, and that we will always remember.

PRESIDENT RONALD REAGAN
at the Dedication of the Vietnam Veterans Memorial Statue November 11, 1984

It's almost 10 years now since U.S. military involvement in Vietnam came to a close. Two years ago, our government dedicated the Memorial bearing the names of those who died or are still missing. Every day, the families and friends of those brave men and women come to the Wall and search out a name and touch it.

The Memorial reflects as a mirror reflects, so that when you find the name you're searching for, you find it in your own reflection. And as you touch it, from certain angles, you're touching too, the reflection of the Washington Monument or the chair in which Abe Lincoln sits.

Those who fought in Vietnam are part of us, part of our history. They reflected the best in us. No number of wreaths, no amount of music and memorializing will ever do them justice. But it is good for us that we honor them and their sacrifice. And it's good that we do it in the reflected glow of the enduring symbols of our Republic.

The fighting men depicted in the statue we dedicate today, the three young American servicemen, are individual only in terms of their battle dress—all are as one, with eyes fixed upon the Memorial bearing the names of their brothers in arms. On their youthful faces, faces too young to have experienced war, we see expressions of loneliness and profound love, and a fierce determination never to forget.

The men of Vietnam answered the call of their country. Some of them died in the arms of many of you here today, asking you to look after a newly born child, or care for a loved one. They died uncomplaining. The tears staining their mud-caked faces were not for self-pity, but for the sorrow they knew the news of their death would cause their families and friends.

As you knelt alongside his litter and held him one last time, you heard his silent message—he asked you not to forget.

Today, we pay homage, not only to those who gave their lives, but to their comrades present today and all across the country. You didn't forget. You kept the faith. You walked from the litter, wiped away your tears, and returned to the battle. You fought on, sustained by one another and deaf to the voices of those who didn't comprehend. You performed with a steadfastness and valor that veterans of other wars salute, and you are forever in the ranks of that special number of Americans in every generation that the Nation records as true patriots.

Also, among the service men and women honored here today is a unique group of Americans whose fate is still unknown to our Nation and to their families. Nearly 2,500 of the names on this Memorial are still missing in Southeast Asia, and some may still be serving. Their names are distinguished by a cross rather than the diamond. Thus, this Memorial is a symbol of both past and current sacrifice.

The war in Vietnam threatened to tear our society apart, and the political and philosophical disagreements that animated each side continue to some extent.

It's been said that these memorials reflect a hunger for healing. Well, I do not know if perfect healing ever occurs. But I know that sometimes when a bone is broken, if it's knit together well, it will in the end be stronger than if it had not been broken. I believe that in the decade since Vietnam, the healing has begun, and I hope that before my days as Commander in Chief are over, the process will be completed.

There were great moral and philosophical disagreements about the rightness of the war, and we cannot forget them because there is no wisdom to be gained in forgetting. But we can forgive each other and ourselves for those things that we now recognize may have been wrong, and I think it's time we did.

There's been much rethinking by those who did not serve

and those who did. There's been much rethinking by those who held strong views on the war and by those who did not know which view was right. There's been rethinking on all sides, and that is good. And it's time we moved on in unity and with resolve—with the resolve to always stand for freedom, as those who fought did, and to always try to protect and preserve peace.

And we must in unity work to account for those still missing and aid those returned who still suffer from the pain and memory of Vietnam. We must, as a society, take guidance from the fighting men memorialized in this statue. The three servicemen are watchful, ready, and challenged, but they are also standing forever together.

And let me say to the Vietnam veterans gathered here today: when you returned home, you brought solace to the loved ones of those who fell, but little solace was given to you. Some of your countrymen were unable to distinguish between our native distaste for the war and the stainless patriotism of those who suffered its scars. But there's been a rethinking there too. And now, we can say to you, and say as a Nation: Thank you for your courage. Thank you for being patient with your countrymen. Thank you. Thank you for continuing to stand with us together.

The men and women of Vietnam fought for freedom in a place where liberty was in danger. They put their lives in danger to help a people in a land far away from their own. Many sacrificed their lives in the names of duty, honor, and country. All were patriots who lit the world with their fidelity and courage.

They were both our children and our heroes. We will never forget them. We will never forget their devotion and sacrifice. They stand before us, marching into time, and into shared memory, forever. May God bless their souls.

And now, I sign the document by which this Memorial has been gratefully received by our government. And now, it belongs to all of us, just as those men who have come back, belong to us. Thank you.

MAYA YING LIN

at the 10th Anniversary of the Dedication of the Vietnam Veterans Memorial November 11, 1992

Oftentimes, I just let the work speak for itself, but I really wanted to come back here for the 10th Anniversary. It has meant a lot for me to have done something that can help so many. I feel I might be the author, but I would like to remain fairly silent. The Wall is designed for you, for everyone to come and bring their thoughts, their emotions to the Wall. You make it come alive. And I want to thank all of you for your service to this country. Thank you very much.

Maya Ying Lin spoke at the Veterans Day 10th Anniversary Commemoration of the Dedication of the Vietnam Veterans Memorial. She designed the Vietnam Veterans Memorial for an architectural class at Yale University when she was 20 years old. She won the open design contest held by the VVMF, and has gone on to become one of the important architects and artists of her generation, designing magnificent and thought-provoking pieces of work around the country.

VICE PRESIDENT ELECT ALBERT GORE

at the 10th Anniversary of the Dedication of the Vietnam Veterans Memorial November 11, 1992

The President-elect is at a Veterans Memorial Service in Little Rock at this hour and I bring you his greetings. I want to also express a word of thanks to President George Bush for coming here last night and participating in the Reading of Names and to Mrs. Bush for serving as the Honorary Chairperson of this event this year.

I want to say on a personal basis it's been hard for me to find the words with which I can come to terms with what Vietnam and the Vietnam War was all about. I bet there are a lot of people in this audience who came home and just didn't want to talk about it at all. And there are a lot of reasons people had for feeling that way, but one of them for me was that it's hard to find the words to describe what it was all about. It's been hard for those of us who served, it's been hard for those who didn't serve, it's been hard for the entire country.

But I do know one thing: this Wall has helped, it's helped a lot. It's helped more than anybody could have dreamed it would have when it was first put up . . .

Veterans, more than anyone else in this country, know that what is important now is the healing process. And may I say as someone in politics, that I believe it's time to put the divisions of the Vietnam War out of our political process once and for all.

There are two special areas of healing that are very important to Bill Clinton and to me and to our country. Number one: we must obtain the truth and the whole truth about every single POW/MIA and we're determined to do it.

As I was walking in here, greeting a lot of folks who reached out their hands, I heard two things more than anything else. The first, of course, was "Welcome home" and others have already said what a special meaning that phrase has. But the other thing I heard was "Bring 'em home," and we're determined to get the truth.

The second special area of healing that must have attention is to have first rate medical care for all our veterans. And again, Bill Clinton and I and this country, we're all determined to make certain that that takes place.

I remember the first time I came here. And just as words are difficult to find, emotions were easy to come by as soon as I saw this Wall. People who are better with words than I am have tried to capture the essence of what it means, and I don't think it can be captured in words. But I know that practically no one could have anticipated that this Wall of black granite would also become a salve, easing pain and offering faith and silently answering unspoken questions. No one could have predicted that this Wall would also become a mirror reflecting the love and hope and unswerving belief in the strength of our American spirit.

No one could have predicted that this Wall of polished black granite would also become a link connecting parent with child, husband with wife, friend with friend, soldier with soldier, connecting us with each other, with our past, with today and with our hopes for the future.

It's now time, in America, to heal those divisions and not just the divisions of a war a quarter-century ago, but also to heal the divisions of wars still raging in our country between different races, religions, communities and peoples. It's time for new hope. It's time for a new beginning. It's time to recognize, as Bill Clinton has said, that we do move up or down with urgency and energy, with courage and compassion, with hope and faith, with respect for the past and an abiding hunger for a future as bright as our dreams.

Welcome home.

GENERAL COLIN POWELL
Chairman of the Joint Chiefs of Staff, at the Groundbreaking Ceremony for the Vietnam Women's Memorial July 29, 1993

I am very, very honored and so enormously proud to be here with you this morning to take part in this ceremony. In a few minutes, the first few shovels of earth will be turned for a monument that has been nine years in the making and over twenty years in the needing.

I want to thank all of the people who worked so very, very hard to make this day possible: First, of course, Diane Carlson Evans, who has given so much of herself to this project for the past decade; of course, Doris Lippman, who served in Japan during that conflict treating burn victims and who has been with this project since 1986; Evangeline Jamison, a veteran of World War II, Korea, and Vietnam; Jane Carson, a 27-year veteran of the Army nursing program; Mrs. Shirley Crowe, our distinguished former First Lady of the Armed Forces of the United States and so many, many others who have worked so hard for this day.

In fighting for this day, you've all performed a tremendous service, not just for the women who served with you during the Vietnam years, but for all Americans. And I congratulate you for this achievement.

When this monument is finished, it will be for all time a testament to a group of American women who made an extraordinary sacrifice at an extraordinary time in our nation's history: the women who went to war in Vietnam.

Over 265,000 women served in uniform during that time, and this monument of course honors all of them. But it honors most especially the 11,500 who actually served in-country and many of you here today were among that group of 11,500.

You went. You served. You suffered. The names of eight of your sisters are etched on the Wall for having made the supreme sacrifice. And yet, your service and your sacrifice have been mostly invisible for all these intervening years. When you finished what you had to do, you came quietly home. You stepped back into the background from which you had modestly come. You melted away into a society which, for too long now, has ignored the vital and endless work that falls to women and is not appreciated as it should be.

I knew you there in Vietnam. I knew you as clerks. I knew you as map makers. I knew you as intelligence specialists. I knew you as photographers and air traffic controllers and Red Cross and USO and other kinds of volunteers. And above all, I knew you as nurses when you cared for those who were wounded and when you cared also, as one of them, for me.

And yet now, almost 25 years after my return, I've begun to realize that I didn't really, really know you well enough. I didn't know what you have been going through all these many years. I didn't know in my heart truly what memories and nightmares you had brought home with you. Only in the past few days have I come to know and to understand what you have been carrying inside. Only in the past few days, have I truly come to understand why this monument is so very important to you and so very important to the nation.

Because, you see, over the weekend as I thought about coming here today, I sat down and began to read a little bit. And on Saturday, I picked up a book of poems, poems that you wrote. The book is called Visions of War, Dreams of Peace, edited by Lynda Van Devanter and Joan Furey. I started just to skim the book to get a few ideas, but what I found myself doing instead was reading the entire book cover to cover, every poem, in one sitting and some poems I have read over and over the last several days. I was overcome. I was transported back over 20 years. I was sharing a time with fellow veterans, women veterans, comrades in arms whose experience I had never fully understood before.

Through your poems, finally, I was listening to you.

I realized for the first time that for male soldiers, the war came in intermittent flashes of terror, occasional death, moments of pain. But for the women who were there, for the women who helped before the battle, and for the nurses in particular, the terror, the death, and the pain were unrelenting, a constant terrible weight that had to be stoically carried. It was a pain that had to be stowed away in a corner of your mind and put in an isolated piece of your heart or you wouldn't be able to continue your work.

The nurses saw the bleakest, most terrifying face of war: the mangled men, the endless sobs of wounded kids . . . not just now and then, but day after day, night after hellish night.

I read other books this weekend. I read interviews you have given. I saw photographs you brought home. To see your strained faces and grim surroundings in 25-year-old snapshots was to marvel again and anew at the strength you displayed.

It's to wonder at: the strength you had to press on; the courage you had to fight to save yet another life; the fortitude to risk your feelings and compassion on yet another wounded soul that might spurn you by dying. It's to feel the invisible wound that you received every time that happened.

How much of your heart did you leave there? How often were you the mother for a kid asking for Mom in the last few seconds of his life? How many 19-year-old sons did you lose?

I didn't realize, although I should have, what a burden you carried. I didn't realize how much your sacrifice equaled and even exceeded that of the men. I didn't realize how much we owed to you then, and how much we should have thanked you and recognized you and comforted you since then. And yet, I see that yours is not a story only of loss and tragedy. It is, as well, a story of inspiration. It's a story of the triumph of the human spirit.

I look into your eyes today; and I see there old pain, yes, but also great wisdom, tempered courage, deep wells of character. I find there the ability to clear the highest hurdles that life can put before any human being, the ability to take on the most terrible truths, and to prevail.

No words of mine can match your own words, and so let me borrow from you by reading a poem written by Lynda. It's called "Making Friends."

Twenty years since my life was changed
Twenty years making a friend of death
Knowing it
Respecting it
Wishing for it at times
Fighting with it as friends sometimes do.

But the nightmares of war have faded as I've healed
My dreams are now of peace
Peace of mind
Peace of heart
Hoping for Peace on earth
It's time I made a friend of Life.

My prayer today is that all of you who were forced at such a young age to make a friend of death have now been able to make a friend of life. The bronze statue that will stand on this spot this Fall will celebrate the hope and the strength, the tenderness and the power, the kindness and the passion that our Vietnam women brought to the struggle for life.

The statue will show three women and a wounded GI, touching each other, giving strength to one another, struggling with mortality, with human emotions, with the pain and exhaustion of both their lives and their spirits.

As part of this Vietnam "circle of healing" which will now be complete, the statue will for all time witness the truth about what you did. There are many scarred but living veterans who will never forget you nurses for helping to bring them back from the brink of eternity. There are many others who are here only in spirit on the sacred Wall who will never forget you, for trying so hard in those last desperate hours.

This monument will ensure that all of America will never

forget that all of you were there, that you served, and that even in the depths of horror and cruelty there will always beat the heart of human love . . . and therefore, our hope for humanity. My fellow veterans—you and your sacrifice will never be forgotten. God bless you all and thank you very much.

General Colin Powell served in Vietnam and later became the first African-American to become the Chairman of the Joint Chiefs of Staff.

SUPPORTING THE VIETNAM VETERANS MEMORIAL FUND (VVMF)

VVMF continues to provide important programs, one of which is to help educate the public about the Vietnam War and the sacrifices of its veterans. This book is part of that vital effort. It will be sent to high schools throughout the United States, free of charge, and distributed to interested individuals. VVMF has other missions as well, including:

- Presenting annual Memorial Day and Veterans Day observances at the Wall
- Providing support and acknowledgment for the Vietnam Veterans Memorial Volunteer Guides
- Providing free name rubbings to the public
- Financing support for Vietnam Veterans Memorial Collection of items left at the Wall
- Inscribing names and status changes on the Memorial (over 250 name additions have been inscribed)
- Storing extra panels of granite for use in case of damage to the Memorial
- Financing engineering research and replacement parts for the Wall and related structures on the site of the Vietnam Veterans Memorial
- Working with Military City Online/ America Online to bring the "virtual Wall" to Internet users (AOL keyword: "WALL"; Internet users: http://www.militarycity.com)

VVMF takes part in other activities honoring Vietnam veterans and educating the public about the Memorial and the Vietnam War on a project by project basis. VVMF is a 501(c)(3) nonprofit organization and its funding comes from grants and gifts from the general public.

If you would like to support the VVMF, please send your tax deductible donation to:

Vietnam Veterans Memorial Fund
1360 Beverly Road, Suite 300
McLean, VA 22101-3685